THE ANDES

STEPHEN LEE

B.T. Batsford Ltd

To Carole and Daniel

A catalogue record for this book is available from
the British Library

Printed in Great Britain by
Courier International Ltd
East Kilbride, Scotland

ISBN 0 7134 6594 8

Frontispiece: Macchu Picchu, Peru.

*Photographs throughout this book are
by the author.*

Contents

List of Black and White Illustrations

List of Colour Plates

(between pages 64 and 65)

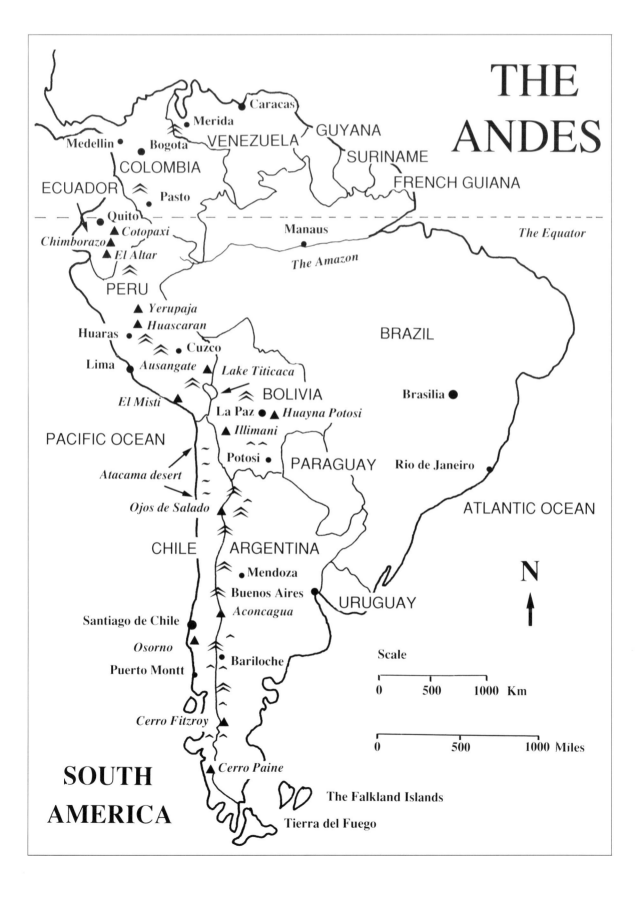

CHAPTER 1 Introduction

The Pirenees, and the Alpes of Italie, are as ordinarie houses [compared to these] Towers.

Father José de Acosta, sixteenth-century traveller to the Peruvian Andes.

The Himalayas may be the highest, the Alps may be the best known and most frequented mountain range, but for pure magic the Andes have few equals. At 7000 km (4,500 miles) from end to end, the Andes would stretch from London to Mexico City or from New York to Hawaii, making this by far the longest continuous mountain range in the world. It is also one of the wildest and most exciting. Despite the ever-present political unrest, even danger, of the South American continent, the Andes continue to attract increasing numbers of adventurous travellers from Europe and the United States.

South America seduces us from afar with promises of train rides across 5200 m (17,000 ft) mountain passes; jeep tracks to ski resorts at 5500 m (18,000 ft); and 240 km (150 mile) long lakes at altitudes not much lower than the summit of Mont Blanc; trekking along Inca routes to the lost city of Macchu Picchu; unlimited opportunities for mountaineering on active and dormant volcanoes; the haunting music of

1. Macchu Picchu, Peru, Lost city of the Incas.

the Andean pan pipes and the colourful clothes and festivals of the Indians.

The seven Andean countries are united only by their mountain heritage. The central Andes of Ecuador, Peru and Bolivia are the most visited parts of the Andes and comprise the major part of this book. The other Andean countries – Venezuela and Colombia to the north, Chile and Argentina to the south – are covered in slightly less detail.

There are two rival explanations for the name Andes. Both originate from the Inca language Quechua. One version has it that the name comes from the Quechua word for metal. The other that it stems from the Cuzco Inca name for the quarter of the Inca empire to the east of Cuzco, *Antisuyo*, which referred to the local mountain ranges. This was picked up by the Spanish *conquistadores* as *Antis*. Eventually, as *Andes*, it was applied to the whole of the range extending all the way down the eastern coast of the continent.

The spine of the Andes (chapter 2) puts the Andes in their geographical context and explains the formation of these comparatively 'new' and, particularly in Ecuador's 'Avenue of

the Volcanoes', still growing mountains. There are many peaks over 6096 m (20,000 ft). Cities at 3657 m (12,000 ft) on and around the Altiplano are not uncommon. Deserts can be flat, hilly or in a valley, such as the Valley of the Moon, close to La Paz. On the peaks and ice-caps huge glaciers, snowfields and uncharted terrain await the adventurer. Elsewhere, montane forest and high altitude *paramo* (moor) are common habitats. There are frequent earthquakes.

The natural life of the Andes (chapter 3) is determined by altitude. Flora and fauna are restricted by the lack of oxygen at high altitude and variable temperatures throughout the year. On the Altiplano the *Puya raimondii* flower

2. Riobamba, Ecuador – 'Sultan of the Andes'.

sports 20,000 blooms. Relatives of the camel in the form of llama, vicuña, alpaca and guanaco are the hallmark of the Andes. The increasingly rare tapir, puma and spectacled bear may also be seen. Andean flamingoes feed on the lakes, hummingbirds dart through the cloud forest and Altiplano – and above them all soars the magnificent condor.

History and exploration (chapter 4) traces the history of the area from the Chavin, Nazca and Tiahuanaco periods through the time of Manco Capac – the Incas – to the Spanish *conquistadores* under Pizarro. Civil war and colonial rule led to the modern period of instability and revolution. Some of the unanswered questions of prehistory are canvassed, such as the conundrum of Peru's Nazca Lines. (Were they the runways of the gods?) Macchu Picchu, the megaliths of Sacsayhuaman and Chan-Chan (the largest clay city in the world) are just some of the magnificent archaeological sites.

The people of the Andes (chapter 5) are of Indian, Spanish and mixed *mestizo* blood. Many Indians retain the traditional dress and lifestyles that are so attractive to the traveller. Colourful markets, Indians who live on floating islands of reeds, the haunting music of the Altiplano and lively local festivals make this a journey to remember. Andean food is sampled country by

3. *Sacsayhuaman, near Cuzco, Peru.*

country. Andean people eat a resourceful blend of fish, meat (from guinea pig to goat) and vegetarian dishes. Local wine is rare but Pisco brandy, coca tea, chicha and excellent local beers offer just some of the unique flavours of the Andes. Two further sections – on music of the Andes and modern living conditions, with the problems of collapsed agricultural economies and the temptations of the cocaine harvest – are included in this chapter.

4. *'State of the art' communications. Quito, Ecuador.*

Visiting the Andes (chapter 6) outlines the best times to go trekking and travelling. There is information on visa requirements and many other useful facts for the traveller. The section on health and personal security takes a look at the many possible pitfalls of Andean travel, ranging from medical problems, theft and terrorism to crossing borders and dealing with black marketeers. The section on mountain dangers deals with the special problems of the Andes. There is advice on wind chill, mountain sickness (*soroche*), hypothermia and snow blindness. Finally, the 'Andes at a glance' section has a factual gazette on each of the seven Andean nations.

Photography in the Andes (chapter 7) looks at

some aspects of high mountain photography. In the Andes, high mountain photography is not only about mountain landscapes, but also about capturing images of local people in the markets, avoiding camera thieves, getting film home safely – as well as all the usual tricks of travel photography.

The Andes by train (chapter 8) picks out the most exciting train journeys in the Andes. The Quito–Guayaquil railway is one of the most spectacular in the Americas; the Cuzco–Macchu Picchu line is one of the best known on the continent. The Juliaca express is the most often held up by bandits; the Bolivian system still runs very much on steam...

Trekking in the Andes (chapter 9) involves walkers either carrying their own gear and food, or hiring a mule and porters, leaving them free to enjoy the scenery. In Ecuador, trekkers can make relatively easy journeys around the Avenue of the Volcanoes. In Peru, the Cordilleras Blanca and Huayhuash provide magnificent walking over 4500 m (15,000 ft) passes, past glacial lakes and through remote valleys. The Inca trail to Macchu Picchu is perhaps the best known trek on the South American continent, while in Bolivia magnificent walks can be enjoyed within hours of the capital, La Paz.

Climbing in the Andes (chapter 10) encompasses all the challenge of Alpine climbing, with the addition of perhaps a few days' walking to reach the base of a chosen climb. Massive ice walls, volcanic snow fields, and myriad unclaimed first ascents still await the adventurer in *Andinismo*. Ten of the best known peaks are described.

6. *Nevado Salcantay, Peru 6372 m (20,574 ft), seen from the Limatambo road, near Cuzco, Peru.*

Skiing in the Andes (chapter 11) is a very different adventure from skiing in the Alps. The few resorts in the Andes are hardly developed at all by European standards, but do offer the unique experience of high-altitude skiing on the Equator. For the off-piste skier or ski tourer the opportunities for first ascents and new routes on skis equal those of the Himalayas.

5. *Market, Pisaq, Peru.*

CHAPTER 2 The Spine of the Andes

THE GEOGRAPHY OF THE RANGE

Geologically speaking the Andes are young mountains. They were formed around 50 to 60 million years ago at about the same time as the Alps. They are high and sharp and comparatively uneroded. A meeting of continental and oceanic plates buckled the earth's crust as the denser oceanic plate pushed under the continental plate to form the Andes. The plates are still closing at a rate of 10 cm (4 inches) per annum.

When continental and oceanic plates meet the oceanic plate generally subsides beneath the continent-bearing plate. This results in an ocean trench being formed close to the edge of the landmass. At the same time the landmass is raised up to form a mountain range parallel to the edge of the trench. Partial melting of the subsiding plate results in volcanic eruptions at points of weakness along the range. This is exactly what happened when the Andes were formed. The collision produced the igneous rock of the Andes to the east and the Pacific trough to the west. The mountains and the trough are today about the same height above and below sea level (6000 m – 19,700 feet). A 12,000 m (40,000 ft) range from ocean floor to mountain peak can be found over a distance of as little as 300 km (200 miles).

Volcanoes are invariably situated along plate boundaries. Active volcanoes are constantly erupting or can erupt at any time. Some volcanoes lie dormant for years but can reawaken. Extinct volcanoes, such as Aconcagua in Argentina, have not erupted in historical times and are not believed to be capable of further activity.

The volcanic activity caused by the plate collision continues into the present day. Ecuador, home of the famous 'Avenue of the Volcanoes' also has the highest active volcano

> **Highlights of the Andes**
>
> The Andes are the longest continuous mountain range in the world, stretching over 7,000 km (4,500 miles) from the Venezuelan highlands to Tierra del Fuego at the southern tip of the continent. It is the world's second highest mountain range, after the Himalayas. The range is slim, ranging from 100 km (60 miles) to 300 km (180 miles) wide in Bolivia. There are 75 peaks over 6096 m (20,000 ft) and some 2000 over 5000 m (16,400 ft). The highest peak in the Western Hemisphere (Aconcagua) is in the Andes, as is the world's highest active volcano (Cotopaxi), and the mountain furthest from the centre of the earth (Chimborazo). Lake Titicaca, at 4556 m (12,500 ft) is the world's highest navigable lake. Also in the Andes are the world's highest city (Potosi) and highest capital (La Paz). The Atacama Desert is the longest in the world.

7. *High altitude* arenal *beneath Chimborazo, Ecuador.*

in the world – Cotopaxi. Many of the highest Andean peaks are of volcanic origin. Currently some 35 South American volcanoes are in a state of major activity. Chile alone has 2000 volcanoes, some 50 of which are active to some degree. Sangay, the world's most active volcano, is in Ecuador. Earth tremors are also frequent.

The Andes run through seven countries. Ten degrees north of the Equator the Venezuelan Andes rise to 5007 m (16,400 ft) and are split into three ranges: the Cordillera de Merida, the Sierra Nevada and the Sierra de Santa Domingo. Colombia has three Andean ranges – the Occidental, Central and the Oriental as well as the separate Sierra Nevada de Santa Marta, rising to 5775 m (18,950 ft). The Ecuadorian Andes,

famous for their volcanoes, are split into the eastern and western Cordilleras; their highest point being Chimborazo at 6310 m (20,703 ft).

Peru's best known cordilleras are the Huayhuash and Blanca, the latter containing Huascaran, at 6768 m (22,205 ft) Peru's highest point. Peru was also the stronghold of the Incas, much of whose heritage is only now being discovered in the tangled montane forest. The Altiplano joins Peru and Bolivia in the Lake Titicaca region, with Bolivia's main peak, Illimani, at 6462 m (21,201 ft). Bolivia lost its coveted sea coast in a war with Chile (the War of the Pacific,

8. *Hamlet beneath the Cordillera Urubamba, on the fertile high plains above Cuzco, Peru.*

1879–84) and is now one of the most isolated countries in the continent.

To the south, Chile, squeezed between the Andes and the sea, has its highest point on Ojos de Salado, 6870 m (22,539 ft). The Andes straddle Chile's long border with Argentina, where most of the highest peaks lie. It also shares the famous lake district with Argentina. Chile has the distinction of being one of the longest (4200 km) and narrowest (180 km) countries in the world, with some of the most varied terrain: snow-capped volcanoes, valleys, the 1000 km (600 miles) long Atacama Desert, fjords, glaciers, lakes and beaches. The Andes occupy between a third and a half of the country's width. Argentina contains the highest

point in the Western Hemisphere, Aconcagua, 6968 m (22,900 ft) and, to the south, the spectacular Fitzroy massif.

Patagonia lies at the southern extremity of Argentina and Chile. Two ice-caps, in the north and south, at an average altitude of 1500 m (5000 ft), are all that remain of a huge ice-sheet that once covered most of the South American continent. Outside the poles and Greenland, they contain the greatest concentration of ice in the world, and are still not fully surveyed. The nearby Paine Horns are some of the lower

Andean peaks, but arguably the wildest and most spectacular of them all.

In the words of the 1930s priest and explorer De Agostini: 'The singular beauty of its fiords, the majesty of its mountains, the imposing vastness of its glaciers, which descend almost to the sea in a green frame of exuberant virgin forest, make of this region one of the most picturesque and enticing quarters of the globe.' As E. Lucas Bridges, borrowing from the first chapters of Acts had it, it is 'the uttermost part of the earth'.

The continental divide

The South American continental divide is only

9. Dry lake bed of Lago Limpiopungo, Cotopaxi National Park, Ecuador.

160 km (100 miles) from the eastern Pacific coast. Most Andean rivers do not run to the Pacific, many go to the Atlantic 5000 km (300 miles) to the east, channelled through the mighty Amazon system. The western Andes consist of a series of batholiths, large masses of solidified magma. Igneous rocks of the western cordillera are relatively resistant to erosion, and the watercourse prefers to leech down through the softer sedimentary rock of the eastern side of the Andes.

Conflicting ocean currents: Humboldt versus El Niño

The tectonic plate collision that formed the Andes and the ocean trough, also resulted in the frigid Humboldt Pacific current, which runs almost the whole length of the Peruvian coast. Cold water is dredged from the depths of the ocean to the surface, which causes moisture to condense over the sea rather than over the arid coastal region and western side of the Andes. Warm land breezes blow on to the cool sea at night and form mist. In the day the mist is blown back in the form of the *garua* – a low level damp mist that covers the coastal strip of Peru from April to September, stretching inland to the foothills of the Andes.

The current is also responsible for the region's most notorious wind – El Niño. Most years a warm current flows south along the Peruvian coast. Since it arrives around Christmas, local fishermen call it El Niño (the Christ child). Every seven years or so, a catastrophic version of El Niño blows, bringing a sharp rise in water temperature and upsetting the balance of the Humboldt current's cold water ecology. The last bad one was in 1983. Inland, monsoon rain brings flash floods, vast landslides wash away railway tracks and roads: natural disasters that these already struggling countries are ill-equipped to deal with.

The Humboldt current also created the longest and driest desert in the world, the Atacama, which stretches for 1000 km (600 miles) along the coast. Temperature inversions mean that some parts of the Atacama have never recorded rain. The desert preserves all – minerals have never been leeched from the surface by rain, delivering nitrate, as it were, on a plate. World climate change has now altered the distribution of rainfall so that the desert does receive occasional rain, putting archaeological sites such as the Nazca lines in jeopardy from the weather.

The Altiplano

The Andes are divided in the middle by the 1000 km (600 mile) long Altiplano (high plain) 3200 m to 4000 m (11,000 ft to 13,000 ft) high that stretches from southern Peru to northern Bolivia between Cuzco and Lake Titicaca. The Altiplano occupies a large part of Bolivia and also includes part of Peru, Chile and Argentina. The Altiplano is home to many of the indigenous people of the Andes as well as to llamas, alpacas and Inca ruins. Higher still than the Altiplano are the *puna* and *páramos* regions (around 4400 m – 14,500 ft) of sparse mountain scenery, with an even sparser population. The forces that created the Andes also created troughs and basins in the high sierra. Volcanic ash and lake sediments infilled the troughs creating the flat Altiplano section, generally poor in nutrients and grazing.

The Altiplano was once covered by two enormous lakes, replenished by the melting of the great ice sheets. Lake Titicaca and Lake Poopo are all that is left. Evaporation is so great that Titicaca can lose 1.3 m (4 ft) of water in a dry season, no mean feat for a lake 240 km (150 miles) long by 160 km (100 miles) wide. The salt flats of Salar de Uyuñi are the best example of evaporation on the Altiplano. About the same size as Titicaca, the salt crust is between 2 m (6 ft) and 8 m (24 ft) deep in salt.

Snow and Ice

The snowline varies tremendously with latitude throughout the Andes. In the central Andes of Peru, Ecuador and Bolivia it may be in the region of 4500 m (14,900 ft) or higher; Peru's Mt Huascaran has the greatest concentration of glaciers in equatorial regions. Down south on the Patagonian ice-cap the snowline approaches sea level, especially in the areas of heavy glaciation.

10. The Sacred Valley of the Incas, near Cuzco, Peru.

Glaciers

Glaciers are born in the gullies around mountain peaks. Layer upon layer of snow building up over time causes pressure that turns loose snow into 'firn' snow (or névé). It takes about 7 m (20 feet) of powder snow to make less than a metre (2 feet) of firn snow. More pressure and melting snow filling in the cavities turns firn snow into firn ice and eventually into glacier ice. The whole process from snowfall to glacier ice takes about five years. Most of the Andean glaciers are in retreat, with the exception of the Perito Moreno glacier in southern Chile.

Avalanche

Avalanches are great dangers in the mountains, especially whenever there has been heavy snow-fall, sudden thaws or after spells of high winds. In the Andes the additional danger of frequent seismic activity acts as a spontaneous trigger to overloaded slopes and causes hanging glaciers to calve massive ice-falls. It does not help that many of the most seismically active areas are snow-covered volcanoes. Natural disasters of this kind punctuate Andean history.

After lying dormant for 400 years, Nevado del Ruiz, Columbia, erupted in 1985, melting snow and glacial ice on the mountain's peak. A wall of mud, ash and rocks slammed through the valleys, uprooting trees and levelling houses, leaving 23,000 dead.

Unpredictable earth tremors can trigger ice avalanches. Peru's Mt Huascaran (6768 m, 22,205 ft) has twice been the scene of a major drama. In 1962 one of Huascaran's glaciers calved a 3 million ton lump of ice about 300 m (1000 ft) from the summit. This avalanched 14 km (nine miles) into the valley, destroying villages and killing 3000 people in the village of Renahirca alone.

Only eight years later, again at Huascaran, a 1970 earthquake (7.7 on the Richter scale) triggered another avalanche that shook loose slabs of rock 60 to 100 m (200 to 300 ft) thick from Huascaran Norte. These crashed onto the glacier below creating boiling mud avalanches (lahars) that hurtled towards the valley on a cushion of air at 300 kph (200 mph). Initially following the 1962 eruption path, these awesome lahars covered 16 km (10 miles) in three minutes. A smaller part of the avalanche jumped the 200 metre (600 ft) high ridge that was thought would protect Yungay. A wave, described by survivors as eight storeys high, crested the ridge and took only seconds to bury the city beneath 10 m (30 ft) of rock, mud and ice. Ironically, the only survivors of the 18,000 inhabitants of Yungay were 240 people who ran up the hill and took refuge in the cemetery.

CHAPTER 3 Natural Life

The natural life of the Andes is profoundly influenced by altitude. The explorer-scientist Humboldt was one of the first to observe this in the early 1800s when he visited the central Andes of Ecuador. Latitude also plays an important part in determining which lifeforms exist and where. Over a mere 300 km (200 miles), Andean terrain can change from Amazonian jungle to montane cloud forest, to permanent snowpeak, to Altiplano, to high moorland, to temperate zones, to hot lowland desert.

It is the high moorland (the *paramos* and *puna*) that defines the high mountain habitat peculiar to the Andes. The *paramos* lie above the normal treeline but below the permanent snowline. In Ecuador and the central Andes (within 10 degrees of the Equator), the *paramos* lie between the *puna* and the snowline. They are windswept, often drenched by rain and shrouded in mist, cold at night and warm in the day only when the sun is not obscured. Cloudy or not, the solar radiation at such altitudes is intense.

There is a sharp division between the eastern and western sides of the Andes. The western is the region of the Altiplano, cold *puna* and *paramos* with relatively limited numbers of species. To the eastern side, the mountains quickly descend into the wet humid jungles, with their profusion of species. The variety of orchids and begonias in the region of Inca ruins is impressive, even around such frequented areas as Cuzco.

The animal and birdlife of the *paramos* and *puna* is by no means abundant, but what is there is conspicuously different from the wildlife of Europe. On the *paramos*, a variety of plants have adapted to the poor soil and harsh climate. In the southern Andes, a lower snowline and generally colder windier weather at lower altitude, allows *paramo* conditions much closer to sea level. Within the *paramos*, terrain may vary from pasture to bog to semi-desert to *arenal*, a sandy desert that joins the snowline and the *paramos*. High-altitude plants and animals tend to reproduce slowly, in order to conserve the limited resources available. Both insects and plants choose dark colours to maximize the intake of sunlight.

FLORA

Mountain plants anywhere in the world have common features. They are generally small so as not to be exposed to the wind and to benefit from the more constant temperatures close to the ground. A roseate structure avoids the leaves shading each other from the precious sun. Downy leaves trap an insulating layer of air, which helps to prevent frost damage.

Other plants have their own methods of survival. The **popa** extracts minerals from other plants. Its seed sticks to the beaks of birds and is rubbed off onto the bark of other trees or spread by droppings. The native **queñoa tree** flourishes between 4000 m (13,000 ft) and 4500 m

(15,000 ft). Here it is superseded by the spiky **ichu grass**, a widespread tussock grass with needle-shaped leaves to reduce its surface area and cut water loss. The uneven growth in tussocks and clumps is hard on trekkers' legs. Ichu grass can only be grazed by llamas and alpacas.

11. & 12. The chuquiraguas plant, with its beautiful orange flowers, is found around 4000 m (13,000 ft) on the paramo. Cotopaxi, Ecuador.

The main exceptions to the general pattern of small plants braced aginst the wind are the great Frailejones and the puyas. Frailejones are quite common on the *paramos* of Ecuador and can be seen in the Cotopaxi National Park. They are a species of *Espeletia*, and are called Frailejones ('Friars') locally because they are big enough to resemble human beings – hence the Friars.

Puyas prefer the drier southern *paramos* of Bolivia and Peru. The best known is the spectacular *Puya raimondii*, named after Antonio Raimondi who discovered it for Western science. They grow to heights of 6 metres and may be a relic of Ice Age flora. The puya is a spiky globe-shaped rosette for most of its hundred years, when it flowers for two to three months before dying. When Puyas do flower, they do it in style. On the stalk, which shoots up from the base of the plant, are 15,000 to 20,000 flowers on some 400 conical spikes, producing up to 10 million seeds.

Puyas dominate the barren land, attracting birds and moths, some of which are caught on the sharp leaves and die. Some scientists argue that the puya is a partly carnivorous plant that makes use of minerals from dead birds and moths. The puya genus, which has over 1500 members and is a relative of the pineapple, is confined to the Andes. *Raimondii* are found only in Peru and Bolivia, under the local name Junco or Llakuash, Cordillera Blanca (Quedabra Pachacoto, in the Huascaran National Park), Chalhuanca and Bolivia west of La Paz.

Often seen on the Altiplano around 4000 m (13,000 ft) is the **chuquiraguas**, which loosely resembles an orange thistle and is claimed to have medicinal properties. It is used as a diuretic and for treating kidney ailments and coughs. They reach about 1 m (3 ft) in height in little bushes with flammable stems and sharp pointed leaves. It is a favourite food of the Andean hillstar hummingbird. The moorland **lupin** (choco de paramo) is well adapted to the bleak climate with its velvety covering that protects it against the extremes of night temperatures and intense solar radiation.

Eucalyptus are widespread at lower levels, but are not indigenous to the Andes, having been imported from Australia in the 1880s. In the lower southern Andes, the heavily forested foothills show a great variety of trees and flowers. In Chile and Argentina you can see **copper beech**, the evergreen **coihue**, and the **arrayanes** with their peeling red bark. The beautiful monkey puzzle trees, once widespread, are now confined mostly to the Chile–Argentina lake district.

FAUNA

The **condor** is the best known Andean bird, a totem for the range from Ecuador to Cape Horn. They are among the largest flying birds in the world, weighing about 12 kg (26 lb). With wingspans in excess of 3 m (10 ft) they glide and soar effortlessly, and have been known to fly away with carrion weighing over 20 kg (44 lb). There is no record of attacks on people, unless as carrion, and they always approach on foot. Andean condors have distinctive white neck ruffs and large silvery-white rectangles on their upper wings. They are long-lived, often surviving 40 years. Close up, it is an ugly bird, clearly a vulture and carrion eater, whose impressive size is masked by the altitudes at which it frequently soars. It is best spotted in flight by its black body, white ruff and spreading wing tip primaries, tracing circles in the sky or soaring above ridges, ascending thermals without flapping a wing.

Young condors do not become sexually mature until their sixth or seventh year. The condors' mating season is July and August, during which the pairs join in a spectacular flying display. Courtship is accompanied by a male 'tok, tok, tok' and a sigh! Condors make their nests on inaccessible cliffs. The single egg is incubated for 40 days. The chick, once aptly described as having 'a face that only a mother could love', spends five months in the nest. The young condors receive help from their parents in scavenging food until their second year. Their slow rate of reproduction together with persecution has resulted in the condor becoming rare. During the 1880s, condors could often be seen in flights of a dozen or so. Now they often fly alone or in pairs. Despite being the 'Andean' condor they are more common by the sea, where there is a better supply of carrion. Cotopaxi and El Altar are good places to see condors, as are the Cordillera Blanca, the Paine horns, or any part of the mountains not frequented by people.

The **zumbador**, the Andean snipe, is named after the strange buzzing noise it makes when it flies, which so often startles the first-time camper to the mountains, since it likes to hide in the day and fly at night. Birds of prey can be seen on the *paramos* – the black chested buzzard eagle, the puna hawk, the cinereous harrier. The distinctive **caracara**, with its orange face and legs, white belly and black back, often scavenges by roads. In the past its feathers adorned ceremonial Inca headdresses.

The **Andean duck** is the most common of the waterbirds in the south. **Torrent ducks** can be seen in fast flowing rivers, where their main food, stonefly larvae, are found. The **Andean gull** has a wide range, preferring moorland with lakes and bogs. It has a black head in the mating season, when it goes to the coast. The **Andean goose** is frequently seen on *paramos* lakes, where **Andean coots** and occasional **giant coots** can also be seen. **Puna ibis** feed in large flocks on the lake. **Andean lapwings** and **speckled teals** are common around the lakes, as are Andean gulls and giant coots.

The over 130 species of **hummingbird** are a common and exciting sight on the *paramos*. About half of the *paramos* plants are pollinated by the hummingbird, and have evolved long flowers that only the hummingbird can reach. Hummingbirds use energy faster than any other animal to sustain a rapid pulse and the muscles that power their wings at up to 80 beats per second. Their wings beat in a shallow figure of eight and enable them to hover and even fly backwards. Some can fly as fast as 70 mph (110 kph). Others such as the rufous humming-bird migrate from Alaska to southern Mexico for the winter. The Andean hillstar is common up to 4500 m (15,000 ft), a remarkable humming-bird whose night time metabolism slows to one-twentieth of the daytime rate, while its temperature drops from 39.5°C to 14°C. The hillstar, at 13 cm (5 in) from tip of beak to tail, is one of the largest hummingbirds, weighing some 20 grams. Others weigh as little as 2 grams.

The **rhea**, similar to the ostrich, is the largest South American bird (1.3 m, 4 ft tall) and fre-quents the grassland pampas of Chile and Argentina. During the breeding season the male marks out a harem of five or six females, preparing the nest with a firebreak of bare earth around it. A modern father, he alone incubates the nest of up to 50 eggs for about six weeks, and rears the young after they hatch. Outside the breeding season, rhea live in groups of 10 to 30. They are swift when running from danger, with a dextrous routine of doubling back and hiding.

Smaller animals

Armadillos are a staple diet in many areas; their shells are made into the sounding board of the Bolivian *charango*, a type of ukelele. The **jambato toad** (jet black with a bright orange belly) is widely distributed in the Andes between 3000 m (10,000 ft) and 4000 m (13,000 ft), par-ticularly in the Cotopaxi Park. They are very active after heavy rain. The **giant toad** of Lake Titicaca grows up to 1 ft (35 cm) long and is edible. The mountain **viscacha**, a rabbit-sized relative of the chinchilla, weighs 3 lb (1.5 kg) and is frequently seen in groups on the high ground below glaciers, where they shelter in scree slopes. They breed three times a year and live from the snowline down to 3000 m (10,000 ft).

Guinea pigs, or **cavies**, are natives of South America. Locally named *cuy*, they are invariably grey-brown in the wild and seem to survive well even at high altitudes. They were eaten by the Incas, who kept colonies of them. The Spanish invaders noticed that the skinned animals looked like little pigs and called them *cochinillo das indas*, or the 'little indian pig'. The prefix 'guinea' was probably added when they were brought by way of Guyana to Europe as pets. Guinea pigs are still considered delicacies and the Peruvian government is attempting to breed bigger specimens as a better food supply.

The **llama** is the quintessential Andean animal. Llamas and alpacas were domesticated soon after the ancient Indians moved to the high plateaux, and their use was integral to the Inca empire. Male llamas can carry about 25 kg (55 lbs) and are still used extensively as pack animals. They are easily herded because each group has a natural leader so only one llama needs to be controlled. They are prone to spitting at their handlers just like their relative the camel. The females are more often reserved for breeding and wool. Both breeds now survive only by domestic breeding. A semi-domesticated herd lives at Cotopaxi National Park in Ecuad-or.

The wild, tall cousin of the llama is the **guanaco**, which lives in family groups of about a dozen. Guanaco came from North America soon after the two continents were joined. The guanaco was never domesticated and was hunted to the point of extinction by the Span-iards for meat and skin. Though they look sweet they can also be quite aggressive and bad tempered. Their wool is an inferior substitute for vicuña wool. Guanaco survive in deserted parts of the Altiplano in small herds of females or bachelor male herds. It is still an endangered species, although numbers are now growing in the Cordillera del Paine and Tierra del Fuego.

The **vicuña**, much hunted for its top quality wool, is also endangered. It uses its speed, an impressive all-terrain 50 kph (30 mph), for escape and long distance foraging. Vicuñas and

guanacos can be seen along the railway between Uyuni and the Chilean border, as well as in Chile's Lauca national park, where they are protected. All these animals which are related to camels are specially adapted to altitude, with an increased number of red blood cells and the ability, through a special stomach reservoir, to go for long periods without water – camels without a hump.

Three main species of **deer** browse the Altiplano – white tailed, brocket deer, and the rarely seen dwarf Andean pudu, which is under 35 cm (1 ft) high. **Puma** are rare, but are occasionally seen around 4000 m (13,000 ft), as is the **Andean fox**. In Chile and Argentina, the **Patagonian fox** is fairly widespread, while the

13. Llamas beneath Chimborazo, Ecuador.

larger **Fuegan fox** (tinged with red and mis-named the Andean wolf) is in decline. **Tapir** inhabit the high cloud forests, with mountain or wooly tapir in the eastern cordillera from 1500 m (5000 ft) to 4000 m (13,000 ft). In the Pappallacta and Sangay regions of Ecuador they are quite common, but are rare elsewhere. They resemble huge pigs with long noses. You may be lucky enough to see the smallest bear in the world, the **spectacled bear**, which is sparsely distributed throughout a wide range from sea level to 4000 m (13,000 ft), preferring the diminishing areas of untouched forest.

25

CHAPTER 4 History and Exploration

The first South Americans came from Asia, by way of the frozen Bering Straits to Alaska, some 30,000 years ago. They filtered down through the North American continent, through what is now Panama into South America. Parts of Peru and Patagonia have archaeological relics dating back 20,000 years. Llamas were domesticated about 5000 years ago, and at this time it is thought that seeds were cultivated, implying the existence of settled agricultural communities mainly based on farming maize. Pottery dating back 4000 years has been found in Venezeula.

About 1000 BC, the Chavin culture emerged on the Peruvian coast, with a developed religious and artistic heritage, whose influence extended as far as the Nazca culture in the second century AD. By AD 300 the Maya indians in Mexico had developed sophisticated civilizations marked by impressive stone temples and hieroglyphic writing. The Aztecs were much later – AD 1200.

There are some similarities between the great Mexican cultures and those of the Andes, suggesting regular social contact between North and South America, but the heartland of early South American history lies in Peru. Ceramic techniques have assisted dating of Mochica pottery (AD 500). The Mochica culture flourished from the third to the eleventh century AD. Their remarkable adobe pyramids can be seen 8 km (5 miles) south of Trujillo (Peru). Also of great interest is the later Nazca civilization (third to eighth century AD), whose 'lines' on the desert have encouraged speculation about extraterrestrial visitors.

THE NAZCA LINES

Four hundred kilometres (250 miles) south of Lima, in the Peruvian desert near Nazca, lie some of the greatest mysteries of the pre-Columbian era. On a flat stretch of desert huge pictures, several kilometres long, of birds and animals have been etched in the sand; a hummingbird in flight, a monkey with a coiled tail, spiders and condors, and less obvious pictograms that seem to conform to strict measurements. Some 30 pictures and designs have been made with rocks and gouges in the desert.

They can only be properly seen and appreciated from the air, and they were drawn at a time when the Nazca (AD 100–800) civilization would certainly not have had powers of flight. The most recent carbon dating puts them around the first century AD. Their purpose is a conundrum that may never be answered. Were they signals or messages to extraterrestrial beings, were they runways for their landing craft? More simply, were they symbolic messages to gods who lived in the sky?

Like Macchu Picchu, the existence of the Nazca lines was locally known, but not fully

14. Young Peruvian sells Coca-Cola under an Inca gateway at Intihuatana, near Pisaq, Peru.

appreciated. A sixteenth-century priest knew of them. In 1926 Peruvian archaeologists were aware of them and pilots observed them in the 1930s. They were discovered for tourism by the New Yorker Paul Kosok in 1941. Since 1948, a German scientist, Maria Reiche, has devoted her life to seeking the key to the riddle of the sands. The answer has not yet been found.

An observation platform has been built to give better views of the Nazca lines, but the best view is from tourist planes, which can be boarded at Lima or Ica. One less encouraging thing seen from the air are the pock marks surrounding the lines, where pre-Columbian graves have been robbed by the *huaqueros* – quite a profitable profession. The rocks that form the lines are also disappearing, and the lines are further threatened by climate change, which in recent years has seen the first drops of rain in the desert. See the Nazca lines soon, before it is too late.

The Chavin culture extended from Pisco to Piura and introduced religious cultism with animal worship and probably pilgrimages. This pre-Inca culture flourished sometime between 1300 and 300 BC, spreading from the coast to the highlands. Its high point was around 500 BC when the impressive Chavin de Huantar temple was built. Stylized jaguars and pumas, eagles and condors feature in the carvings that can still be seen in the underground ruins at Chavin, some 35 km (21 miles) from Olleros in Peru, and 80 km (50 miles) from Huaras. The later Inca masonry may be impressive, but these carvings are some of the best in Peru and rival the Aztec and Olmec sculptures of Mexico.

TIAHUANACO

At Tiahuanaco, Bolivia's most important archaeological site, the famous Gate of the Sun shows traces of the Tiahuanaco culture. It is clearly pre-Inca, but the civilization that created it disappeared in the eleventh century AD. Some evidence points to the existence of Tiahuanaco

as early as 1600 BC, but the best evidence we have suggests that their territory extended from northern Bolivia to the Ayacucho area of Peru, flourishing between approximately AD 800–1200. The ruins are in the process of reconstruction in four parts – the Kalasasaya compound, the Acapana pyramid, the underground temple, and the Gate of the Sun. The Incas knew nothing about them, beyond that they were an older civilization. Now some distance from Lake Titicaca, it is believed to have once been on the shores of the lake. The Gate of the Sun may have been a solar calendar. Less impressive than Macchu Picchu, it still gives an insight into the heritage of the Bolivian indians – the Aymara.

The Gran Chimu, based at the walled city of Chan Chan on the northern Peruvian coast, was the most artistically advanced of the pre-Inca civilizations. The Chimu culture extended from Lima to Piura in approximately AD 1000–1500, during which time Chan Chan, the largest adobe (mud) city in the world, was built by the coast near what is now Trujillo in northern Peru. By AD 1500 the Chimu culture had been effectively absorbed into the Inca empire.

CHAN CHAN

Chan Chan, meaning Sun Sun, was situated 4 km (2½ miles) to the west of the modern city of Chimu, and was founded by a mythological character called 'Tacaynamo'. The Chimu empire once extended from Tumbes to Lima. In its heyday, Chan Chan was some 20 sq km (8 sq miles) with perhaps 250,000 inhabitants. Some 14 sq km (5.5 sq miles) are left and it is now completely uninhabited. It was built about the twelfth century AD and flourished until the fifteenth century. Chan Chan was invaded and conquered (but not looted) in 1460 by the Inca Pachacutec, after which it fell into disuse. The Spanish, however, broke open the burial mounds of the kings and looted silver and gold ornaments.

In 1925 and 1983 Chan Chan suffered major floods, and has been ravaged by earthquakes and treasure seekers over the years. Despite this, many fine examples of marine-inspired designs carved in high relief in the clay can be seen, such as seabirds, crabs, octopi, lobsters, sea otters and geometric designs. Chan Chan was divided into nine walled palaces, each one built for a king. It is the largest known city to have been constructed entirely of clay. It has largely been preserved by the dryness of the Peruvian coastal climate – it may not survive if climate changes bring more rain.

THE INCAS

The Incas are possibly the greatest posthumous tourist attraction of today. Since we have so few facts about them we can use our imaginations to fictionalize their magical heritage. Even the experts admit that, in the absence of written

15. *Inca houses as they might have been. Stonework and thatch near Pisaq, Peru.*

history before the arrival of the Spanish, our knowledge of the Incas and others is sixty per cent guesswork, thirty per cent probability, and ten per cent established fact.

Their very name and language is the subject of misrepresentation. There probably never were a people called the Incas. The 'Inca' was the Quechua name to describe just one person, the supreme ruler. Lacking a word for the Inca's subjects history has lumped them together under the word 'Incas'. Also, Quechua is really the language of an unknown pre-Inca tribe. Many prefer the real name Runasimi. Neither language had an alphabet, and only the Spanish interpretations from 1532 and the modern language of today's Indians remain to help us piece together a picture. So history records the 'Incas', who spoke 'Quechua'.

17. *Main square, Cuzco, Peru.*

Nor were the Incas an inventive people. They simply used the skills of conquered tribes. The Inca's greatness lay in their capacity to unify and organize under their central leadership. The trapezoid stonework, perfectly joined without modern tools, is an enduring legacy. Stonework that was not destroyed by the Spanish has survived untouched by earthquakes, which is more than can be said of the *conquistadores'* constructions.

In the eleventh century AD, a small tribe from the valleys north of Lake Titicaca began a conquest of the mountains, subjugated the powerful Chimu kingdom of Chan Chan and swept down to the coast. They probably originated from the Cuzco area, and a number of legends have sprung up about their arrival. One has it that the Sun, taking pity on the Barbarian living in darkness, sent his son, Manco Capac, to Earth, while the Moon sent her daughter, Mama Occllo, to be Manco's bride. They rose from the waters of Lake Titicaca and travelled

16. *Cuzco, Peru, the Inca 'navel of the earth', the Spanish mountain capital.*

to Cuzco, where they claimed that the Sun God Inti commanded them to found a capital on the place indicated by a shaft of light. This was Cuzco meaning 'Navel of the Earth'. The Andes were sacred mountains to the Incas. Whenever they climbed a peak or pass, an offering was made to its spirit.

The Incas were the first people of South America to have a concept of a nation, and this is why the modern but disparate South American 'nations' often hark back to the Incas with nostalgia for a unified South America that has not been seen since. The kingdom of the Incas spanned most of the Andes and what it did cover was unified under a workable system. At their zenith their empire stretched over 3500 km (2200 miles) from the Ecuador/Colombia border at Pasto to the Rio Bio Bio in Southern Chile, where the ferocious Araucanian Indians halted their expansion. East to west they were really a coastal and mountain people. It was a narrow empire, extending from the coast through the Andes to the eastern edge of the mountains.

The Incas called their empire Tawantinsuyo, the Four Quarters of the Earth, with Cuzco as the navel. To the north lay the Chinchaysuyo – northern Peru and Ecuador. The west was the Condesuyo, the south central coastal regions. South was the Collasuyo, the Altiplano of southern Peru and Bolivia. To the east was the Antisuyo, where the mountains met the jungle. The Spanish name Andes comes from the Inca name for the inhabitants of the Antisuyo region east of Cuzco – the Antis. At first it was applied only to the mountains east of Cuzco, but later to the whole range.

Cuzco's location was ideal for the Incas' capital. The coastal area was barren, but agriculture flourished in the high valleys around Cuzco. The town was captured by Pizarro in 1533. It suffered major destruction after a siege in 1536 when the Incas threw red-hot stones on the city's thatched roofs and burned their own city to the ground. The Spanish capital was later moved to Lima. Cuzco moved out of the limelight, except for the occasional earthquake and the nearly successful revolt led by the Inca Tupac Amaru. This reached an abrupt end when he was torn limb from limb by Spanish horses in Cuzco's main square in 1572. A modern day revolutionary movement, MRTA (Moviemento Revolutionario Tupac Amaru), has taken his name.

Cuzco again rose in importance when Hiram Bingham, an American explorer, discovered Macchu Picchu in 1911, but it was not until 1948 that the site was made more accessible to tourists by the construction of a road from Aguas Calientes. The modern tourist era has made Cuzco one of the most visited cities in South America.

Macchu Picchu

It is possible that the Spanish may have known about Macchu Picchu but soon abandoned it. The Incas withdrew further into the mountains where they were harder to find and could mount guerrilla-style attacks on Spanish supply lines. It is also likely that local Indians knew of the site continuously from the time of the conquest until 1911, when Hiram Bingham's National Geographic/Yale expedition 'discovered' the site for modern science and for tourism. Bingham coined the phrase 'The lost city of the Incas' in his book on the discovery and exploration of Macchu Picchu. This description has captured the world's imagination and made Macchu Picchu the unquestioned first choice of any visitor to South America, Peru and the Andes.

Perched on a plateau above the thundering Urubamba River, with precipices, montane jungle forest, hummingbirds and orchids to every side, the site has all the magic and mystery one could desire in a far-off dream destination. Allied with the well preserved buildings, it is easy to step back in time, put yourself in the Inca's sandals and imagine the life of these wild and proud people who worshipped the sun and the seasons. Macchu Picchu was a flourishing ceremonial and agricultural city. The distinctive Inca masonry supported the cult of the sun and the coca leaf, which in those days was the preserve of the nobility.

The Inca empire worked because it was a dictatorship with strong leadership, well organized and fitted to the Andean terrain. Life was hard but bearable. The well-maintained culverts and fields were well kept, ensuring bountiful harvests and freeing labourers to build and maintain the empire's roads. Travel was not allowed, except on official business, so that people stayed on the land and did not flee to the cities as today. When a man could no longer work because of age or illness, he knew that he would still eat and that the community would look after him.

18. Macchu Picchu, Peru.

Other Inca ruins

The area around Cuzco is a confusing mass of steep montane forest, where perhaps many other Inca sites remain undiscovered. Just around the bend of the Urubamba from Macchu Picchu lies a recently discovered site, Killapata. The site is two kilometres (a mile and a half) long, clinging to a cliff with agricultural terracing, aqueducts and warehouses. Ceremonial sites, perhaps even male mummies, may be unearthed from its graves. The site when fully excavated could turn out to be even more important than Macchu Picchu.

In their 150-year heyday the vast Inca empire, on a par with the Romans, produced remarkable stonework and fed its subjects three times over – all without a written language or the wheel. Their main strength was organization and skilful colonization by using the local skills of the conquered and re-settling conquered tribes in new areas to spread the unifying Inca language of Quechua. The 'Inca' was the supreme ruler, and everything in Inca life was channelled to serve the 'Children of the Sun'. They in turn provided their subjects with a totally controlled safe society, more than can be said for modern South American countries. Life was hard but predictable for the Inca worker, working to produce the potato or quinoa crop, with one-third of the food for the people, one-third for the Inca, and one-third stored for the Sun God.

Sacsayhuaman

Half an hour's walk from the city of Cuzco is the vast ruined cult centre of Sacsayhuaman, one of the finest examples of Inca masonry. Each July it is the setting for a re-enactment of the Inca Festival of the Sun. The impressive technical achievements – 300 tonne blocks of stone joined almost seamlessly – and its commanding location overlooking the capital of Cuzco made it appear rather fortress-like.

Recent discoveries of priests' graves make it more likely that this was, in fact, a religious centre. The 360 metre (1180 ft) long ramparts face what is now thought to be the Inca's throne and altar. Ingenious small watercourses running all round the stones are now thought to be 'chicha grooves', where the alcoholic home-brew ran in the religious festivals – a sort of draught chica. On another hill are a number of smooth straight grooves sculpted 50 metres (150 ft) long in the rocks. They are now thought to be rock slides for children to play in. Nearby are seats cut into the rock for parents to watch. It seems that it was not all hard work in the Inca empire. The huge size of the individual rocks and the sheer scale of the site as a whole make this one of the most impressive archaeological sites of South America.

Inca stonework

Despite having more advanced technology, and having already built superb buildings of their own, the Spanish were most impressed by the first examples of Inca stonework they saw in the Cuzco streets, the fortress of Sacsayhuaman, the sacred valley of the Incas, Ollontaytambo, and the many superb examples of Inca masonry in the area.

Inca stonework has been variously described as the work of demons, magic, magical herbs, even 'extraterrestrials', but the reality was perhaps more prosaic. A few basic tools, massive manpower and an understanding for the raw materials combined with a religious fervour inspired by strong leadership and endless patience to produce this superb work. The only scientific skills the Incas had were perhaps the inclined plane; the log roller; possibly pulleys; the patient use of hard hematite stone; wooden wedges that expanded when wet; and crafty use of small pebbles to hold open cracks in the split stone. Horizontal, load-bearing joins always fitted perfectly, while upright ones were often filled with rubble and mud, suggesting that

19. Sacsayhuaman, near Cuzco, Peru.

labour saving, not magic was the order of the day. The preferred modern view, advanced by Peter Frost's excellent book *Exploring Cusco*, is that all of the above factors contributed to the impressive stonework we see today.

The Incas did not write. Their main legacy was their stone buildings and roads. Roads and tracks traversed the mountains for transport and defence. At the peak of Inca supremacy in the region, 20,000 km (12,000 miles) of Inca footpaths and trails traversed the empire, so that nowhere was more than five days' journey from the capital, Cuzco. Cuzco to Lima took 72 hours by specially trained runners, the *chasqui*.

In the absence of a written language, messages were relayed by *quipus*, lengths of knotted llama strings, gold for gold, silver for silver, red for military intelligence. *Tambos* or inns were spread along the trails at about 20 km (12 mile) intervals. The runners could make about 10 kph (6 mph), blowing a conch as warning of their

20. Detail of stonework, Sacsayhuaman, near Cuzco, Peru.

arrival so the next runner could prepare. Each community was responsible for the upkeep of the roads in its area, and for river bridges, made from twisted *maguey* fibre, which had to be renewed each year. Today trails such as the Inca and the Takesi trails can be walked by travellers. Thousands of kilometres of stone pathways through the Andes still remain to be opened up. Fortresses occupied the key points in the Inca network of roads.

At its height the Inca empire stretched over Ecuador, Peru, Bolivia and partly into Argentina and Chile. Their expansion was halted, as were the Spanish later, by the Araucanian Indians around the Rio Bio Bio in Chile. The Inca population has been variously estimated at from one and a half to eight million, the latter figure being supported by comparatively recent discoveries as to the productivity of their agricultural methods. The expansion that began in the twelfth or thirteenth century AD was, as is often the case with empires that grow too unwieldy, the beginning of their downfall. When the empire was split between the sons of the Inca, Manco Capac, it was already in the grip of a civil war. Then came the Spanish.

THE SPANISH CONQUEST

Deeply in debt, both financially to her creditors and spiritually to the Catholic Church, sixteenth-century Spain was the most powerful kingdom in Europe. Taking quick advantage of the immense possibilities of the New World seemed the answer to all Spain's prayers. She was not disappointed. In Mexico, Hernán Cortés, with just 500 men and 16 horses, had conquered the Aztecs in just two years. Meanwhile, in the Andean Inca empire, the Inca, Huayna Capac, had split his empire between his sons, Huascar and Atahualpa. Civil war quickly ensued. By 1532, when Pizarro landed with 180 men and 27 horses in Tumbes, northern Peru, the Inca empire was ripe for conquest. The Incas had never seen horses and were terrified by the mounted cavalry – even more so when a soldier dismounted. At the battle of Cajamarca, Atahualpa was captured and the Spanish held him to ransom. The Incas filled a room full of gold, but in vain – the Spanish took the gold and killed him anyway. They went on to take Cuzco, after which the Inca empire rapidly disintegrated. The last Inca stronghold was overrun in 1572, when the Inca, Tupac Amaru, was executed. It is estimated that in the first 50 years of Spanish rule, the Inca population declined by as much as 75 per cent.

Separate expeditions by Mendoza to Argentina and Valdivia to Chile meant that by the middle of the sixteenth century, Spain's conquest of the New World was mostly complete.

Their colonial reign was to last for 300 years. The continent was split into the viceroyalties of New Granada (Colombia, Venezuela and Ecuador); Peru (Peru and Bolivia); La Plata (Argentina) and Chile. Lima was the capital of the empire, befitting Peru's status as the richest country in South America and the one to be most plundered for gold and precious metals. All exported goods had to pass through Lima and thence to Panama for taxation before shipment to Spain.

The countryside and its people produced little that was valued by the Spanish and they were largely ignored. The Spanish army had arrived womanless and mixed freely with the local Indians, creating the *mestizo* races that now populate most of South America. Where convenient, Indians were enslaved and made to work in appalling conditions down the mines. The *criollo* (creole) class and *peninsulares*, the first generation of locally-born Spanish, firmly held the balance of power.

Spain bled the continent of raw materials, and sold back processed goods at high cost. Resentment flourished. The dominant *criollos* – merchants and bureaucrats – resented interference from the motherland. Meanwhile, the local Indians increasingly resented the powerful *criollo* dominance of their land and people. In 1780 a rebellion was led by the Indian army of Tupac Amaru, a descendant of the eponymous Inca, amazingly in the name of the Spanish king. It was mercilessly stamped upon by the local *criollo* forces, but the seed of revolution was sown.

In the early eighteenth century, revolutionary movements, fuelled by trends towards democracy in Europe, gathered speed under the flag of Simón Bolívar, who won battles in Caracas and Bogotá and eventually reached Guayaquil in Ecuador. Further south, San Martin won victories for the revolution in Chile and occupied Lima. In a mere 17 years, an empire that had stretched from California to Cape Horn, from the Orinoco Delta to the Pacific, had

21. Spanish colonial spire of the Archbishop's palace, Quito, Ecuador.

royalists in Ayacucho (Peru) in 1824. Southern Peru seceded from the old viceroyalty, calling itself Bolivia, after Bolívar. Gran Colombia split into Ecuador, Colombia and Venezuela, giving us roughly the modern boundaries of the Andean nations. The rout of the Spanish left a power vacuum, leading to lawlessness, looting and anarchy. Bolívar despaired, declaring that 'America is ungovernable, and . . . will inevitably fall into the hands of a mob gone wild, later to fall under the domination of obscure small tyrants of every colour and race.'

The failure of any concept of South American unity was underlined by the failure of the conference of Panama in 1826, when only four countries attended. Those who did attend were clearly only interested in their new-found territories. Such has been the pattern of modern times in South America and the Andes.

The first 60 years of South American independence from Spain is a history of civil war, strong military rule by *caudillos*, with the *criollos* and *peninsulares* in clear control of the Indian and *mestizo* majorities. In 1879, Chile's powerful navy defeated Peru and Bolivia in the War of the Pacific, annexing part of Bolivia, which lost its sea coast in the process. Bolivia's navy has been confined until today to Lake Titicaca.

Even after the Spanish were ousted the exploitation continued. The developed world manoeuvred to get a foot in the door of the South American strongroom, bursting as it was with minerals and natural resources. The British began to exert a real influence on trade by building railways in Chile and Peru. The Americans became heavily involved with trade in Peruvian *guano* and later nitrates. These were over 30 times more effective than farmyard manure and both were used to fertilize the farmlands of Europe and America. Since 1823 the US had attempted to enter the arena by taking advantage of the loose wording of the Monroe doctrine. This stated that the US would not tolerate any European attempt to interfere with the South American continent, which was

dwindled to just Puerto Rico and Cuba. The European independence movement, the seizure of Spain by Napoleon, the increase in UK and US trading interest in South America – all of these contributed to the ousting of the Spanish.

THE MODERN PERIOD – AFTER THE SPANISH

The Spanish were gone, but what was left? Attempts at a unity of purpose by the two liberators Bolívar and San Martin ended in failure. Bolívar went on alone to defeat the more correctly, they claimed, linked with North America.

Later, Roosevelt expanded the terms of the Monroe doctrine, stating that the US reserved the right to interfere internationally wherever its own interests were threatened. This began a period of US gunboat diplomacy, that has continued to the present day. In 1904, at the prompting of the USA, Panama seceded from Colombia, creating the republic of Panama. Behind this lay an American desire to protect its interests in the canal, which was finished in the same year.

By the early twentieth century, the USA had eclipsed the UK in South American trade, developing Venezuelan petroleum and Chilean copper. Two world wars distracted foreign interest in South America, which continued to grow economically without outside interference. Later the Cold War and the Cuban missile crisis of 1959 brought north-south relations into the modern era. The 1960s and the 1970s saw increasing north-south interdependency.

The USA and other countries have increasingly become involved, by way of aid programmes, in local South American issues such as drugs, terrorism and politics. South Americans tend to view foreign aid in any shape or form with suspicion, believing that it usually entails a partial surrender of local control. Indeed, *El Norte* (as the South Americans call the USA) is often blamed for creating the problems in the first place that the aid is supposed to cure.

This is typified by the drugs problem in Colombia, Peru and Bolivia. The argument goes that if there was no demand for cocaine, the agricultural communities in South America would not be growing coca as the most profitable crop. Therefore, US intervention in the form of coca crop defoliation and financing antidrug armies would be unnecessary. A solution seems as far away as ever. Since the murder of the ransomed Atahualpa, foreigners have never really been trusted in South America. The

Roman Virgil, writing about the Trojan Horse said, 'I fear the Greeks, even when they bear gifts'. So it is with South America. History cannot be rewritten.

Venezuela

Venezuela bore the brunt of the fighting in the war of independence from Spain. After independence it sank into relative obscurity. Its natural resources were not exploited. There followed years of anarchy, corruption and internal fighting. Internationally, there was a dispute with the UK about the frontier with British Guiana, leading eventually to a blockade in the early 1900s by the UK, Germany and Italy in an attempt to secure repayment of loans. Venezuela's fortunes soared in 1917 with the discovery of oil, and by the end of the 27-year long Gomez era Venezuela had paid off all her foreign debt.

Agriculture suffered widespread neglect during the oil boom and despite Venezuela's enhanced international standing, country people were as poor as ever. Between 1945 and 1958, a succession of military coups followed by elections gave Betancourt two periods of office, enabling some oil money to be ploughed back into the local economy. Less reliance on foreign investment has resulted in Venezuela becoming one of the more stable Andean countries in recent years. Carlos Andres Perez was elected for a second period of office in 1989.

Colombia

From 1812 to 1819, the liberator Bolívar fought a campaign of mixed success until the decisive victory at Boyacá (1819) enabled him to enter Bogotá and state emphatically that independence had been won. Colombia spent most of the nineteenth century in a state of civil war with the government continually changing hands between the Conservatives and the Liberals. The poorer Colombians fared no better than before independence. The dominant *criollo* class did little for the indians, the *mestizos*, the blacks or the mulattos. In 1899 the political conflict brewed into a civil War of a Thousand Days in which 100,000 people died. In 1904 the USA took advantage of the confusion to foment a secession movement in Panama, then a Colombian province, which eventually became an independent state in 1921. The prize, of course, was the opening of the Panama Canal.

The War of a Thousand Days paled by comparison to the carnage of the period, from 1948, known as 'la violencia'. Three hundred thousand died in the struggle between Liberals and Conservatives. Relative peace followed a power-sharing agreement under the Frente Nacional. This lasted until 1986, when the Conservatives refused to participate in the government of the elected liberal Virgilio Barco.

Two major problems are firmly ingrained in modern Colombian society – drugs and guerrillas. Guerrilla movements have flourished since 'la violencia' of the 1950s, and the main movements, FARC, M19, ELN and EPL, have now formed a worrying coalition, the *Coordinacion Nacional Simón Bolívar*, against the government. Meanwhile, Colombia continues to be the main processor of coca leaves into cocaine *en route* to the USA and Europe. Eighty per cent of the world's production takes place here. In the 1970s the highly organized Medellin cartel took over production from small localized units.

The drug barons own huge factories in the jungle, run their own hotels, newspapers and armies, as well as providing more prosperity for local people than the government ever could. At one stage, in search of amnesty, the drug barons offered to pay off the entire Colombian national debt. Since 1984, the government has declared war on the trade, yet, despite American assistance, the drug problem is likely to remain a source of violence until a legal but more profitable alternative crop can be found.

Ecuador

Ecuador split from the short-lived Republic of Gran Colombia in 1830, and for the next century had a similar history to her neighbours. Struggles between Liberals and Conservatives, military coups, lack of strong central government resulting in collapsed industry and agriculture – these left the population wondering what had been gained by independence. The Colombian frontier was not finalized until 1916, and is still disputed. Meanwhile, in 1941, a long-standing disagreement with Peru over the ownership of part of its eastern jungle region, the Oriente, erupted into a war in which a large part of the region was lost to Peru. This was never accepted by Ecuador, and hostilities were re-kindled in 1980. This area, clearly marked on modern Ecuadorian maps, is now closed to tourists.

A democratically-elected government has been in power since 1979, and the country, like Venezuela, is relatively stable by South American standards. The main economic problems have been caused by the vagaries of the oil price – Ecuador's main export – and by the devastation wrought by the 1983 *El Niño* and the 1987 earthquake. Otherwise, Ecuador is a calm and tranquil destination for the visitor.

Peru

Bolívar dealt the *coup de grâce* to the Spanish at the battle of Ayacucho in 1826. Short-lived governments interspersed with military interludes dominated the next fifty years, culminating in Peru's humbling defeat at the hands of Chile in the War of the Pacific (1879–1882). It was not until the early 1900s that Peru began to raise its head again.

The *hacienda* system was the main Spanish agricultural legacy to South America, a system whereby land snatched from the Indians was given to *peninsulares* and worked under a system of virtual slavery. Peru has the largest Indian population in South America, mostly resident in the mountains. The Indians have survived into the present day almost completely unintegrated into the modern world of the

22. *Pisaq market, near Cuzco, Peru.*

coast. Modern *campesinos* have no Inca, no leadership, and worse agricultural conditions than in the Inca period. Meanwhile, the larger cities, especially Lima, are surrounded by shanty towns of refugees. They have abandoned the now bountyless Pachamama, mother earth, for an even poorer life of urban destitution, for which neither their heritage nor their government has prepared them.

The return of land to its original owners was long the objective of the APRA party, and by 1968 this was achieved after a military coup under Alvarado. US oil companies were nationalized, farmers organized collectives, but progress was again halted by another coup in 1975. Agriculture was starved of finance, *campesino*

dissatisfaction ran high, and the stage was set for the growth of Sendero Luminoso.

The Sendero Luminoso (literally, the 'Shining Path') have taken advantage of rural poverty and discontent to set up a revolutionary movement that since 1980 has been responsible for a number of bombings, attacks on public officials, fund-raising robberies, and latterly a pledge to 'bring down the Peruvian state'. Almost half the Peruvian departments are under a state of emergency, and as we go to press the British Foreign office is recommending that visitors avoid these areas. Some tourists have been caught up and killed by the indiscriminate actions of Sendero Luminoso. The Túpac Amaru group (MRTA) have also come to the fore in the last decade and have been responsible for recent bombings and kidnappings.

APRA returned to power again in 1985, but the general instability of Peru, problems with terrorism, drugs, and national debt have discouraged any foreign investment apart from tourism, leaving the Peruvian state rudderless into the 1990s. Elections were disrupted in late 1989, but Alberto Fujimori, a Japanese-Peruvian, gained power for the Cambio 90 (Change 90) minority party, inheriting a legacy of a shattered economy and a ten-year guerrilla war. The Peruvian currency, the Inti, is weak, while the army remains strong and almost above the law. Fujimori's government has played into army hands by declaring the capital, Lima, an emergency zone under martial law, along with almost half the country. For Peru the nineties may be a decade of change, but although the players' names may be different the problems remain the same.

Bolivia

After the conquest of the Tiahuanaco culture by the Incas, the main development was the Spanish invasion and the mining of silver from Potosí. The colonial period was one of slavery and exploitation, but independence did little for the people except give what was once called 'Upper Peru' a new name after the liberator Bolívar – Bolivia. From independence to the present day, the tone of Bolivia's political life can be guessed by the fact that in 161 years there have been 80 changes of government, mostly by military coup. One week in the early 1980s was christened the 'week of the seven generals' by virtue of the seven changes of head of state in that period.

Weak government affected the borders. Bolivia was unable to control neighbouring states. In 1879 it attempted to tax proceeds from nitrate mining in the Atacama Desert, to which Chile responded by annexing a valuable part of the Atacama Desert leading to the War of the Pacific. Bolivia lost its sea coast, which to date is often claimed but has never been regained. Brazil annexed part of the rich Acre area in 1903. Paraguay took part of the Chaco in the war of 1933–5. In all cases Bolivia was 'compensated' with the building of railways – some still operational, some never completed, some of which have run into disuse. Bolivia has never had a great deal of international clout: Queen Victoria once crossed Bolivia off the map when she was offended by it!

Chile

Valdivia was the first Spanish governor of Chile. He founded Santiago and other central cities, but failed to advance further south than the Rio Bio Bio, stronghold of the staunch Araucanian (Mapuche) Indians, who had also defeated the Incas. The Mapuche, hunter-gatherers without a central leadership, were widespread throughout Patagonia. The Spanish were unable to deal a decisive blow by capturing or killing the Mapuche leader – there was none.

On the contrary, it was the Mapuche who routed the Spanish by killing Valdivia. Two versions of his death exist; one, that they passed his head around on a pike, second that molten gold was poured down his throat – a taste of Spanish medicine. The Mapuche were the only South American Indian tribe that learned to manage horses and devise military tactics that were effective against the Spanish. Between 1599 and 1604 all Spanish settlements south of the Rio Bio Bio were destroyed by the Indians and had to be abandoned.

Post-conquest Chilean society was set up on the basis of *encomiendas*; soldiers were given land and Indians to work them. Since Valdivia's expedition brought only one woman, the soldiers quickly interbred with the natives, and the new Chilean race was born. Land grants created the farms and were the basis of modern Chilean society. Even by the 1950s, the majority of the land was concentrated in the hands of very few in *encomiendas*, farms or *fundos*, as they are locally known.

After independence from Spain, O'Higgins, despite his foreign name, became the new head of Chile. Although he made many excellent reforms, he did not kow-tow sufficiently to the all important landowning classes and was overthrown by the military in 1823.

At this stage Chile was smaller than today. Natural resources, especially nitrate and copper, were abundant in the north of the country. Their presence attracted foreign investment and a new form of colonial trade interference, which, more often than not, led to war. The British-trained Chilean navy won the War of the Pacific (1879–82), annexing the nitrate-rich Atacama Desert from Peru and Bolivia. Nitrate, used for fertilizing US and European farms, was the mainstay of the Chilean economy for 40 years. The Mapuche Indians were finally subdued in 1883, bringing Chilean Patagonia under central government control.

In 1891 Chile was plunged into civil war after the Balmaceda regime's unsuccessful attempts at social reform. Foreign investment (by the US, the UK and Germany) was the key for the first part of the twentieth century. After World War II only the US remained active in Chilean investment, as the UK and Germany nursed their post-war wounds. Heavy US investment followed in the 1950s and 1960s.

Chile in the 1970s saw the Allende years end in general strikes and the inevitable coup, leading to the Pinochet regime. There followed 16 years of murder, repression, torture, purges of the left and the widespread 'disappearance' of anyone who posed a real or imaginary threat to the dictatorship. The *desaparecidos* ran into the tens of thousands. The Aylwin era began in 1989 when the 70-year-old was elected to power. Even with the end of repression, and the regaining of free speech, it is hard to see how the people of Chile get by with an average wage of $60 (£45) per month, but these are the facts of life for modern Chile.

Argentina

Although San Martín liberated the viceroyalty of La Plata from the Spanish in 1821, real internal freedom did not come until 1853 after a series of civil wars. A constitution, inspired by that of the USA, was then adopted. In the 1860s when the US was engaged in civil war, the UK turned to Argentina for its agricultural products. The grassland pampas of Argentina became the source of much of her future prosperity. In the late 1800s, Argentina's population multiplied as the country actively encouraged settlers from Europe to tame and farm the grasslands. In the process vast numbers of local Indians were dispossessed and killed. By the Indian Wars of 1878–83 most of the pampas were in the private ownership of the few, being worked, as in the rest of South America, by the many. By 1906 three out of four inhabitants of central Buenos Aires were European-born.

The first hundred years of independence followed the familiar pattern of exchange of power between Liberals and Conservatives, interspersed with military power seizures, culminating in the rule of Perón from 1946 to 1955. Peron's first period of office delivered a number of improvements in the daily life of the average Argentinian. His glamorous wife, Eva, shared in his glory and in a fair bit of the financial success of the era. She was idolized after her death in 1952.

Peron was overthrown by the military in 1955. The civilian Frondizi government (1958–62) gave way to more military rule until 1973, when Peron again came to power, with another glamour girl, Isabel, at his side, as vice president. After his death, she became president in 1974. In the following years the country was ravaged by terrorism, vigilantes, disappearances, kidnappings and lawlessness, not to mention inflation at two per cent a day. The military

coup in 1976 ensured the continuation of the violence.

Two devaluations left a previously over-valued currency in ruins, and by 1982 salaries fell to ten per cent of their 1976 value and the military junta, desperate for a distraction from internal problems, launched the ill-fated Falklands war, based on an 1833 claim to the Islas Malvinas (Falkland Islands). They lost the war and the junta was overthrown, returning Argentina in 1983 to a civilian government. The *desaparecidos*, the thousands of civilians who had disappeared under military rule, were dead. Those responsible were prosecuted by the new leader Alfonsín, the sheet being wiped clean by a pre-election amnesty. Carlos Menem is the current Peronist leader of Argentina, whose task is to deal with the hyper-inflation that has again overtaken the country after the loss of the war and the discredit of the military government.

THE LEGACY OF HISTORY

The Spanish conquest of South America pro-

23. *Quito, Ecuador ... a sandwich of cultures. An advert for the Schwarzenegger film 'Sobreviviente' ('Survival') looks down on the street graffiti publicizing Amnesty International and a populace in chains.*

duced enormous wealth for the Spanish, but left a legacy of confusion. The Inca empire and their way of life were destroyed. Their terraces fell into disuse and their intricate mountain roads and irrigation systems were overgrown by the lush montane forest. Much of Inca history is lost to us because of the absence of a written record. It is hard to see what the Spanish gave in return. Theirs was a policy of plunder – when they departed they left many social problems and few local institutions in place to tackle them. Despite 'independence' from Spain, power still rests to a large extent with the *peninsulares*, the descendants of the *conquistadores*.

The problem of modernizing any society without totally destroying its roots remains unsolved in South America, as elsewhere in the world. Travel and tourism are facts of life and

24. *Buildings old and new. Adobe buildings in the foreground; Inca stonework of Sacsayhuaman, near Cuzco, Peru, in the middle distance.*

cent to as much as 1000 per cent. Here, in the 'first world', ten per cent inflation is a crisis. In South America it would be considered 'as safe as Inca stonework'.

1992 is the 500th anniversary of the conquest. Modern Spain has retitled this rape of a continent 'the encounter between two worlds'. Today the inhabitants of the New World wonder how the Old World can celebrate a process of invasion, colonization and genocide.

The progress of South American independence was wisely charted by the liberator Simón Bolívar. At first he talked of 'the sweet agitation of freedom' and how the greatest wish of a people was 'the glory of living under laws dictated by their own will'. Finally he came to realize that 'he who serves the revolution here is ploughing the sea. South America is ungovernable.' Ironically, the vacuum left by the defeat of the Spanish was filled by the military, the *caudillos*, a legacy that South America is only now sloughing off in favour of shaky democracy. As democracy gains a gradual toe-hold in South America, the modern era has become the twilight of the generals.

Historically, the richest exports of the Andes have always been the downfall of her countries. Gold, silver, tin, nitrates, guano, oil, cocaine have all brought wealth to the few, trouble to many and frequent invasion, military or economic. Instability is the result; the poor stay poor, ripe with dissatisfaction and hungry for revolution.

The daily lives of those outside the money economy – the *campesinos* of Peru, Ecuador and Bolivia (perhaps over half the populations) – remain largely unaffected by five hundred years of history. All the passage of time has achieved is to make their traditional agricultural life less workable. Village life founders as families are split by terrorism, disappearance and the demoralizing flight to the cities.

All in all, history has left the real people of the Andes – the dispossessed original owners of the land – poorer by far.

history, but almost every foreign footfall leaves a mark or scar on indigenous cultures. Some aspects of racial destruction are obvious – war, conquest, genocide, even unwitting slaughter, as with the Fuegan Indians, practically wiped out by the introduction of measles and the common cold.

South America is still an unknown continent. Even its name is uncertain. Columbus called the inhabitants 'Indians'. Spain called the land the 'Indies'. Europeans coined 'America'. After independence the French called it 'Latin America', while the British stick to 'South America'.

Further cancers attack these societies. The seven modern Andean countries are faced with annual rates of inflation ranging from 200 per

CHAPTER 5 People

'May the blight of our superior civilization never fall upon them.'
– W. H. Hudson – The Purple Land *– 1885*

The Andes pass through rich lands that are full of poor people. The people are of Indian, Spanish and mixed (*mestizo*) blood. Many Indians retain their traditional dress and lifestyles, which are so attractive to the traveller. Colourful markets, Indians living on floating islands of reeds, the haunting music of the Altiplano and lively local festivals make the Andean journey one to remember.

Indigenous tribes, be they of Quechua, Aymara, Inca or other origin, have rarely survived unaffected by modern life. The Spaniards quickly dismembered the Inca empire. There followed a period when the blood of the new and old worlds was mixed irreversibly. After the Andean countries gained independence from Spain, what was left was a mixture of mixtures.

In some parts of the Andes the descendants of the *conquistadores* purged and exterminated the local Indian population. Even now to describe someone as an Indio is an insult. In these societies all things chic and European are the modern aspirations and there is little left of the pre-Columbian heritage. In other countries the strong Indian tradition has been carried forward into the present day. *Campesinos* (local Indians) with their huge lungs, hearts and barrel-chests are well adjusted to a strenuous high-altitude life on the land. They continue to farm with the same methods and often on the same terraces as their Inca forebears. They keep the same fiestas (albeit with a pagan version of Catholicism). Their weavings, music and handicrafts are the delight of visitors. This, perhaps the greatest living heritage of the Incas, is largely what travellers come to see in the Andes. The modern Indian tradition, not completely coincidentally, is at its purest in the most visited countries of Ecuador, Peru and Bolivia.

South American life is fragile. Four per cent of Chilean children die before reaching the age of one year, 13 per cent in Bolivia, 9 per cent in Peru. Average life expectancy in Chile is 68 years, Bolivia 51, (unless you are a miner, when 35 is the norm), and 58 in Peru compared to about 75 in most developed nations.

VENEZUELA

Ninety per cent of the country's inhabitants are crowded into one tenth of the land, the northern Andean and coastal belt. The highlands and the Sierra Nevada are sparsely populated. This is the best place to encounter Venezuelan Indians, dressed in their colourful *ruanas*, the local name for ponchos.

COLOMBIA

25. Pisaq market, near Cuzco, Peru.

The Spanish and Indian influence is predominant, followed by that of the Negro. Before the Spanish conquest the country that is now Colombia was inhabited by Indian tribes. The population is now about 60 per cent *mestizo*, 14 per cent mulatto, 20 per cent Caucasian, 4 per cent Negro and 2 per cent pure Indian. Racially Colombia resembles Brazil, with a very mixed population of *triguenos* – mixtures of white, black and Indian. Coastal people are of Caribbean stock, while the pure Indian breeds are found in remoter parts of the country such as the Pacific coast and the Santa Marta highlands.

Colombians have the worst reputation for *machismo* in South America and violence is never far below the surface. Political power is still largely concentrated in the hands of descendants of the *conquistadores* and some of the better qualified immigrants. They are popular targets for ransom demands by the drug barons. The most popular crop is coca, which has given the *campesino* a standard of living far higher than any traditional crop could ever do.

ECUADOR

26. *Market traders, Latacunga, Ecuador.*

The population of Ecuador is approximately half *mestizo* and half pure Indian. There tends to be a greater mix in the larger urban areas while in the high country areas the pure Indian race and way of life is more in evidence. In these areas, Quechua is widely spoken. Indeed, ten per cent of the population speak only Quechua in local villages where life has hardly changed in centuries. Spanish is sometimes spoken as the second language. Until very recently *campesinos* were almost completely outside the money economy, eking a poor living out of the land in the Andes, or working under near-slave conditions for the owners of large *haciendas*. They had very little contact with the modern *mestizo* world. Tourism has been the joining factor – it is after all the Indians who are interesting and not the cities, which are poor imitations of our own. Some groups, such as the Otavalo Indians have become well organized at selling their attractive weavings to tourists. *Campesinos* are starting to form small co-operatives or collective farms but still live very much at subsistence level. Only literate Indians can vote, and since most of the Indians are illiterate, they have little political clout.

The Otaveleños can be recognized by their white calf-length trousers, their rope sandles,

grey or blue ponchos and a long single braid of hair. The Salasaca men wear distinctive broad-brimmed hats, white shorts and black ponchos. The Saquisilí Indians are often seen wearing red ponchos and little felt hats.

27. Mother and child, Latacunga, Ecuador.

Otavalo's Saturday market is perhaps the best place in the Andes for buying genuine and distinctive local crafts, such as ponchos, bags, weavings, rugs, sweaters, baskets, etc. Many of these are also found in the shops of Quito but quality is poorer and prices higher. Do not be afraid to bargain in markets – a little polite bartering is expected. The Otavaleños are quietly spoken businessmen with a talent not only for weaving but also for making a good living. Saquisilí near Ambato is also impressive for the variety of tourist weaving as well as a substantial produce market that seems to fill every street and plaza. Fiestas and markets are a major part of the Indian heritage, an excuse to throng in from the hills wearing their traditional finery.

Although Quechua and Aymara Indians often inhabit the same villages, their languages share no common strain. Quechua was the Inca language, so Quechua-speaking Indians are today found wherever the Incas ruled. It was Inca policy to establish Quechua-speaking settlements in their colonies. The Aymara Indians and their language are today found mostly around Lake Titicaca, which they hail as the birthplace of man.

An even rarer Ecuadorean Indian tribe are the Tsachilas Indians of Santo Domingo de Los Colorados. Their main settlement, Chihuilpe, is only 100 km (60 miles) from Quito in lush tropical jungle, at a mere 800 m (2400 ft) altitude. Their name (*Colorado* means 'coloured') comes from the red paprika colouring (*achiote*) that they use on their hair and clothes and with which they stripe their bodies. The warm climate enables loin-cloths to be worn, while the isolation of their jungle habitat meant that their lifestyle remained unchanged until very recently. Inevitably, many Indians have now

28. Mother, child and llama, near Cuzco, Peru.

adopted Western clothing but their traditional attire is still seen at the Sunday market of Santo Domingo de los Colorados. If you take photographs, they will expect to be paid.

PERU

The Spanish conquest of Peru obliterated the traditional Inca world. A few years of war and occupation was all it took for the delicately balanced agriculture and mountain irrigation of the Incas to be lost for centuries. *Campesinos* became slaves to the Spanish and the Inca empire was bled of its gold. Indians in Bolivia and Peru were forced to work in the mines. In 1780 Túpac Amaru led an unsuccessful rebellion against the Spanish which was mercilessly crushed. But the seeds of later independence had been sown. The Peruvians of the high

country continued to farm, while the better-off *peninsulares* continued to dominate politics and business. Modern Peruvian families are often huge. Ten children are not unusual in the countryside, with the first born when the mother is just 13.

As one would expect from such a tourist Mecca, Cuzco is also a good place to buy local weavings, and every variety of poncho, sweater, multicoloured socks, etc. is on offer. Colours tend to be more garish than that of Ecuador. In the Cuzco area, do not miss the craft markets of Pisaq and Chinchero, in the Sacred Valley of the Incas.

BOLIVIA

Some three-quarters of the Bolivian population live on the Altiplano. About fifty per cent of Bolivians are descended from the Aymara or Quechua Indian cultures. One-quarter is *mestizo* and one quarter white. The country is ruled by a white minority who refer to the Indian

29. *Cuzco, Peru.* Campesino *in the city.*

population as *cholos, campesinos*, peasants or *mineros*. Many Indians are abandoning their traditional ways, apeing the dress and social customs of the ruling minority. After the Spanish had squeezed Peru and the Incas dry of gold, they turned to the silver that was discovered in abundance in Potosí in Bolivia. *Campesinos* were sent to work down the mines in appalling conditions, most were dead by the time they were 35, a life expectancy that has continued into the modern period. When the silver ran out, the tin mines took over as the stick with which to beat the *campesinos*.

Now that the mines have been nationalized, some minimum standards have been set, but the average life expectancy of the miners has not changed. Silicosis pneumonia is still the most likely cause of death. Miners live in tied accommodation. When a miner dies his family has to leave unless another member of the family is also working in the mine. Altiplano life, seen from a Western standpoint, is almost unbearably hard. The land is mostly too poor for successful agriculture. Migration to the cities is the sad end for some of these once proud people. Many Indians, speaking Aymara and Quechua, had no vote until 1952 because they were illiterate. Hardly surprising that they intentionally dull the effects of altitude, poverty and deprivation by chewing coca leaves and indulging in bouts of drunkenness on homemade *aguardiente*. Recently the processing of the raw material of coca leaves has led to a new industry and source of income – cocaine.

Cholos is a name for *mestizos*, half-Indian half-Spanish blood, but it is also a name for those *campesinos* who have moved from the country to the city. Bolivia is also home to a number of expatriates: Germans, Mennonites and Japanese all form small independent minorities. Bolivia has the world's lowest gross national product. The average Bolivian earns about $350 per annum. Despite this, those living outside the money economy have a relatively bearable subsistence existence.

About three quarters of the population live on the Altiplano, and despite the hardships, they refuse to move – it is Pachamama, Mother Earth, their home. The worship of Pachamama is well adhered to in Bolivia. A visitor to the Witches' Market (Mercado de las Brujas) of La Paz will encounter many seemingly ghoulish relics, such as dried llama foetuses. These are a modern substitute for the sacrifice of a live llama, which returns to Mother Earth what was taken from her. Burying a waxed llama foetus under the foundations of a new building or enterprise guarantees a successful outcome, or so goes the belief.

The reed boats of Lake Titicaca

One of the most intriguing groups of Aymara Indians are to be found on Lake Titicaca, on the islands of Suriqui and Ouros. These are floating islands of reeds, on which small communities of fishermen have lived for a millennium. The reeds are the stuff of life. Their houses are reed shacks constructed on the floating island. A few islands are large enough to boast a football pitch. During the game the terrain bounces and sways like a drunken mattress. Some of the weeds growing in the shallows are even edible.

Last but not least come the boats. Reed boats are made from the tortora reed, sometimes equipped with reed sails. Such is the expertise of the local boat builders that four islanders from Suriqui were selected by Thor Heyerdahl to construct the 11 m (36 ft) ocean-going *Ra II*. Its object was to prove that the ancients of the Mediterranean could have crossed the Atlantic and discovered the Americas before the Spanish.

ARGENTINA

The Argentine population is a very different racial mix to that of the northern Andes. The population is almost completely European, most of the Indian population having been exterminated in racial wars during the nineteenth century. Notable are the Argentine gauchos, whose mastery of the horse played a great part in the taming of the pampas to the east of the mountains. The Quechua word meaning orphan ('*wahcha*-vagabond') is the origin of the word gaucho. It alludes to the loneliness of these solitary men herding cattle on the pampas, living off beef, maté tea and *aguardiente* liquor.

CHILE

Chile is very European-American in character, population and culture. Large numbers of German and Swiss immigrants intermarried with the Spanish colonials, making the latter less dominant in the modern racial mix and power structure. The Indian population was enslaved to work on the huge ranch estates (*estancias*) of the landowners. Only about three per cent of the current 12 million population are indigenous Indians. The Chilean equivalent of the gaucho is the *huaso*. Darwin compared the two: 'The gaucho may be a cut-throat but he is a gentleman; the *huaso* is an ordinary vulgar fellow.'

In southern Chile and south-west Argentina, the modern bustling commercial city of Temuco contrasts with the neighbouring Araucanian (Mapuche) Indians, who still proudly preserve their traditional ways of life. Fiercely warlike, they were the only South American Indians to have successfully resisted the Incas and the Spanish. Unlike the Incas, they were quick to master the horse. The last resistance of the Mapuche to foreign rule was not suppressed until the late 1880s. The Spanish soldier and poet Alonso de Ercilla was so impressed by the Araucanians that he composed a poem, 'La Araucana', to their bravery;

> *They are confident, emboldened*
> *Dauntless, gallant and audacious,*
> *Firm inured to toil and suffering*
> *Mortal cold and heat and hunger.*

Few Araucanians now remain in the south of Chile, dispossessed from their own land in the familiar fate of aboriginals the world over.

In 1833, when Darwin visited these latitudes, there were some 8000 indigenous Indians (Yahgans, Tehuelche and Ona) in the southernmost Andes near Tierra del Fuego. They lived in wigwams and hunted with bows and arrows. Incredibly physically resilient, they thought nothing of hunting naked in the snow. Relying heavily on the guanaco for food and fur, their guanaco moccasins earned them the nickname 'Patagones' (big feet), hence the modern name of the southernmost part of South America – Patagonia. The smoke from their fires gave rise

to the name Tierra del Fuego. They were no match for the white colonists of the 1870s. Within a short time many had died of measles or had been shot as vermin. By 1947 only 150 survived. Now the tribes have died out and the fires of Tierra del Fuego have been quenched.

LIFE IN THE ANDES

Modern village life

The 'modern' Andean or Altiplano Indian village is often collectively owned. Daily life is organized on the basis of reciprocity. Money does not change hands, but large jobs such as building houses are done communally. Backpackers who come to a village should ask permission to enter from the mayor, the *gobernador*, often recognizable by the staff he carries. Indians, treated with respect, will often be very hospitable. The mutual help basis of Indian society, dating back to Inca times, is constantly threatened by the very presence of travellers. *Campesino* children often beg as a matter of habit, *da me propina* (give me a tip) being a common request. It is tempting to give a few coins but it is better by far to exchange some goods, needles, pictures, food, etc. In this way both sides keep their respect and the *campesinos* are not dragged further into the vortex of the money economy, for which they are completely unequipped.

Dress and traditions

It would be wrong to infer that every Indian encountered on a South American journey will be dressed in exquisite hand-woven costumes. Outside special occasions, American/European clothes have become the norm for many people, particularly agricultural workers, who may just wear a simple poncho and hat on top of jeans, sweater and sandals. *Campesinas* (*campesina* women) are more traditional. It is not unusual for a woman to wear three or four skirts at the same time, with the most recently washed one

close to the skin. A *manta* is worn by the women around the shoulder, and no *campesina* looks dressed without the almost obligatory baby poking its head out of the back of the *manta*, nestled into the fruit and vegetable purchases from the market. Tourists are often sold machine-made substitutes of the traditional hand-woven ponchos. The traditional weaving process is time-consuming and tedious, and less attractive than turning over a quick profit.

The bowler hats worn by many Andean women, especially by the Aymara of Lake Titicaca, are a conundrum. Apparently the Spanish King Carlos III forced them on the Indians as part of a conformity drive. Trilby hats are found in north Peru and the Cuzco area, while flat black hats with tassels are worn by the older women. Despite the colonial connotations, headwear is essential so high above sea level and so close to the Equator. Indian women are rarely seen hatless.

30. Hand spinning, near Cuzco, Peru.

Religion, *Apus* and Pachamama

Modern religion in the Andes is a mass of contradiction. The Spanish *conquistadores* claimed South America first for God and second for Spain. Indeed the Catholic religion was an essential part of the *conquistador* power base. They believed that the pagan Indians would not be saved by God if they were not converted to Catholicism. This they did by a mixture of coercion and persuasion. Rogue priests were among the first to speak out for human rights on behalf of the Indians. Today Catholic churches are scattered throughout the Andean region and are well attended. The Christian God and pagan deities are worshipped side by side. Holy week in South America is as fervent and fanatic as in Seville. Now 90 per cent of

54

South America is Catholic. By the end of the century, it is estimated that more than half the world's Catholics will be South American. The Mormon Church is gaining ground there, too.

It may have been that the jungle-living Jivaro Indians did indeed shrink heads and that the Incas did make human sacrifices. But the *conquistador* version of history may have emphasized the barbaric pagan nature of what they found to justify their crusade of conversion. Traditional objects of worship have never disappeared – llama foetuses are still commonly used to bring luck to a building or enterprise. Worship of the sun, moon and the spirits (*Apus*) of every natural formation is still ingrained in Indian consciousness.

Mother Earth is called *Pachamama* in Quechua, the Inca language. She lives and nourishes Man and allows him to cultivate her. She is happy and sad. In a mixture of the old and new religions, she dies in Holy Week and is

31. Mother and child, Pisaq, near Cuzco, Peru.

reincarnated. Andean Indians make offerings to her at different times, and her permission is asked before ploughing or planting the earth. The bond between *campesino*, the earth and the environment is the basis of life in the mountains; the *Apus* (spirits) of man, the rivers, clouds, mountains and earth are as one. Where 'progress' has taken over the Indians have lost their closeness with the land, and the link with Pachamama is gone. What is left is a pagan form of Catholicism. A massive statue of the 'Virgin in chains' overlooks the city of Quito. Christ looks down on the great Inca city of Cuzco, his back turned on the ramparts of Sacsayhuaman, where each June/July the Sun God Inti is worshipped in full pagan splendour as the *chicha* and the blood of llama flows. Clearly the true inner beliefs of the Andean

32. *Christ above Cuzco, Peru.*

Indian cannot be encompassed within the framework of a single recognizable religion. One commentator summed it up nicely when he said that in South America Catholicism left the people who worshipped the sun holding mere candles.

Music of the Andes

The musical imports to the South American continent and the Andean regions have been many and various. The true music of the Andes, however, is the music of the indigenous Indian population of the mountains and the Altiplano.

Music is one of the most enduring legacies of the Inca civilization. Many Aymara and Quechua names are still used to describe Inca instruments that are in use in modern form. Today musicologists accept that the Inca and Spanish traditions are inextricably woven. Song and dance are indistinguishable in Indian conception: the Quechua word *taqui* describes both. Early Inca music was often the music of war. The Incas were said to make flutes from the leg bones of their defeated enemies. *Conquistadores* and missionaries did much to stamp out the indigenous music and dance used in religious festivals, fearing it might act as a call to arms:

'We shall make a drum from his skin,
We shall make a necklace of his teeth
We shall play the flutes of his bones
And we shall drink from his skull.'

33. *Mother and child, Latacunga market, Ecuador.*

This song was collected by the Peruvian folklorist Farfan in 1940, and echoes the writings of Waman Puma from around 1600.

In time the Indians responded to the Spanish influences, and were quick to adapt new forms to old tunes. Hence the *charango*, resembling a miniature guitar from the front, with the sounding board made from the shell of an armadillo. Relatively modern hybrid though this is, it has now become one of the distinctive sounds of the Andes. The haunting sound of the panpipes had its origin in Inca times, and is still heard in the Andes today.

Not all songs were songs of war, and love songs filled the air as they do today. The great *Raymis* (Inca celebrations/fiestas) were where the songs were most heard, as they still can be today in the spectacular setting of the Inti Raymi in Sacsayhauman in Cuzco. The lack of range and notes available in most sets of panpipes means that the average band of players, especially in the Altiplano bands of Titicaca, number over a dozen in order to incorporate the full range of notes required.

Inca music was heavily stylized. Singers and flautists often numbered in their hundreds. Male musicians came from the helper or servant class, while a special class of 12-year-old girls sang in the high falsetto still typical of the Cuzco region. The guitar has been incorporated into the traditional bands seen plying the streets. The range of the Andean harp is limited by only having 36 strings, but at least it is portable for street festivals.

The true range of Andean music is roughly the former range of the Incas, from south-western Colombia down through Ecuador, Peru and Bolivia into Northern Chile and Argentina. It is the music that expresses most accurately the harshness of life in the high mountains and on the barren Altiplano. It is particularly poignant in view of the demise of the proud Inca nation at the hands of the Spaniards. In the highlands the *yaravi* and the *huayno* are the most common songs. The *yaravi* is Quechua for lament and sings of lost love, death and the struggle against adversity. The *huayno* has a happier theme, with slow and fast sections.

For the impoverished Altiplano dweller, music is the acoustic equivalent of chewing coca leaves. It gladdens the spirit and diminishes the hardships of life. Major displays are often a part of the new tourist heritage, while the simpler songs of the remote villages may feature just one or two instruments in a monotonous repetition of basic musical themes. The traveller's best chance of hearing authentic Andean music is at a *peña*, which may be a simple tavern or an expensive night club. Andean music at its best is harsh and unsophisticated. It has a harmonic resonance that quickly becomes addictive. Years later, a few bars of quivering panpipes can pluck you from the streets of London and deposit you in a reed boat floating on the shallows of Lake Titicaca, snow peaks sparkling in the thin air.

Fiestas

Many Indian dances at fiestas are symbolic of religious beliefs. Traditional dress adds considerably to the spectacle. Well known festivals are Inti Raymi, the festival of the Sun God Inti (June/July in Cuzco), the Virgen de la Candelaria (Lake Titicaca, 2–10 February), and the Raqchi folk festival.

Fiestas are common occurrences in villages. There will always be one on the day of the village's patron saint as well as many others. Do not miss the chance to witness or even join in with any fiestas you encounter: dancing, masked semi-pagan processions, grotesque Yawar condor fiestas, the great fiesta of Inti Raymi at Cuzco and the Racqui folk festival among countless others.

Pachamama is not always kind. People barely scratch a living from a land ravaged by floods, drought, earthquakes, volcanic eruptions, terrorism, highway robbery, widespread social injustice and unemployment. Despite this, the *campesinos* show a remarkable spontaneous ability for enjoyment and spectacle. Their respect for heritage puts our own 'comfortable and civilized' Western world to shame.

The Festival of the Sun – Sacsayhuaman

Each July sees the festival of the Sun and Moon at Sacsayhuaman, a re-enactment of the most probable use of this impressive site above Cuzco. From his altar throne, the 'Inca' presides over traditional Inca dancing and singing, complete with symbolic llama sacrifice. The chicha flows freely down the rock channels of Sacsayhuaman. Modern *campesinos* reach drunkenly for their lost heritage while the Inca tradition is played out for modern tourists to the whirr of a thousand motor-drives and video cameras.

The Raqchi folk festival

Similar ethnic ecstasy can be seen at the Inca folk festival in the Peruvian town of Raqchi. This celebration of Indian music brings spectators from all over the Andes, with dancing, panpipes, *charangos*, chicha and all the spontaneity of the Indian blood.

The Yawar fiesta

29 July, high on the Peruvian Altiplano, is the Day of the Condor. The condor symbolizes the indigenous Indians, the Incas, the original owners of the Andean high land. The *campesinos* go to a secret place in the mountains. A horse is killed as bait and they wait. The condors come. They feed and feed till they are engorged and can barely fly. Now the *campesinos* strike, easily netting a bloated condor. Paraded around the village, its bravery and strength are toasted in chicha.

A bull, symbol of the *conquistadores*, is brought to the Plaza de Armas. The condor's feet are sewn with leather thongs to the shoulders of the bull. A ghastly struggle ensues. Blood flows freely as bull and condor go mad with rage. The bull usually collapses with exhaustion and dies. The Indians celebrate the spilling of blood as a sacrifice to Pachamama, spirit of Mother Earth.

Symbolically, this rewrites history – the Incas have routed the Spanish. Túpac Amaru, the last defeated Inca, will reward them with fertility and a good harvest. The village drowns in drunkenness and celebration for two days, when the condor, once more anointed with chicha, is released back to its more peaceful mountains. It is no surprise that the fiesta is outlawed by the authorities, not only for what it symbolizes, but for the cruelty both to bull and condor.

Another equally gruesome Condorachi fiesta takes place in the Callejon de Huyalas, near Huaras in Peru. This involves punching a condor to death in a form of horseback jousting. The dealer of the fatal blow has the apparently great honour of biting out the long yellow tongue of the condor.

Fiestas can be seen in a number of contexts. First and foremost, they are fun, and a break from the harsh routine of *campesino* life. Second, they are a search for something lost. One senses a longing for a national identity. I am not referring to the identity of being a Peruvian, a Bolivian, etc. Passports are merely the modern manifestations of an aboriginal land carved up into political slices by invaders. Rather, the modern *campesinos* search for an identity as being part of a greater, nobler race – the Incas, the lost identity of the continent. To this end, the Inca 'flag' has been invented in recent years and is often seen flying at Inca/Indian folk/ethnic festivals. It links today's Indians to a more glorious past before the white man came.

THE DRUG ECONOMY – SOUTH AMERICA'S WHITE GOLD

Andean agriculture, livelihood of the *campesino*, has been ravaged by storm, flood, earthquake, terrorism, government instability, lack of foreign investment and unemployment. Unseasonal frosts have wiped out maize harvests – the last straws to break the *campesino*'s back. Many have deserted Pachamama and migrated to shanty towns on the outskirts of the cities. Those who stay put have to scrape a living in any way they can.

Coca leaves, the raw material of cocaine, grow luxuriantly in the South American climate of the montane forest, where the Andes meet the jungle. In some countries they are grown legally. Leaves are chewed to minimize the effects of altitude and generally to numb the senses, or are made into coca tea. In Colombia,

Bolivia and Peru the production of cocaine has reached such huge proportions that it is the largest single export of these countries. Even ordinary peasant families are finding they can make ten times their normal income by cooking up a *pasta* of coca leaves for sale at about US$7 per kilo to a middleman, who will sell it on for US$12 per gramme. When it reaches Miami, Los Angeles, London or Frankfurt it may fetch $100. The income generated for the average *campesino* gives the only hope he has ever had of rising above his rural poverty, buying a truck, and being somebody.

The authorities are ambivalent. On the one hand the cocaine trade is tolerated, on the other they say to the USA and other Western powers, which create the market, that they are attempting to stamp out production. The reality is that the trade will not be stopped until a crop or resources of equal value can be substituted for the coca leaf. In parts of Colombia, whole valleys and towns where the local drug barons organize and police their trade with private militia and extensive bribery are 'no-go areas' for the authorities. For the locals in coca producing areas, the employment situation has never been better and there is no disincentive to continued production.

It is thought that some 60 per cent of the world's cocaine is produced in the Huallaga valley of Peru, 30 per cent in Bolivia. Most of the processing is believed to be done in Colombia. As much as a third of the Bolivian economy may be financed by the trade, while Peru's coca industry has a suspected $900 million annual turnover.

International efforts, spearheaded by the US, have been made to curb the coca trade and substitute alternative crops for the 100,000 Peruvian and 50,000 Bolivian growers. These attempts have ranged from widespread defoliation raids on crops to the use of coca products for non-addictive wines, beauty products and weight loss potions. As to the effectiveness of the latter, Americans are sceptical. Coca growers make about $3000 per annum per hectare (2.5 acres); coffee makes $800 and rice $600. The economics are obvious.

Meanwhile in Peru the problem has been compounded by the terrorist group Shining Path, Sendero Luminoso. Apart from tending to undermine government authority, the intrusion of American Green Beret anti-drug units is seen as yet another gringo invasion of the Andes. American intervention results only in the guerrillas gaining more support from the local populace whose livelihood depends on the coca crop.

A recent seizure of 270 kg (600 lb) of cocaine in Madrid showed the boldness of the Colombian traders. Each package was sealed with the label '100 per cent pure, product of Colombia'. Meanwhile, back in Colombia, the drug barons have been accused of attacking all who oppose them. It is said that judges and leading politicians have been shot; newspapers who speak out against them are bombed; elections are disrupted; aircraft are blown out of the sky. The fear engendered by Colombia's narco-terrorists has resulted in a lawless society, prowled by the *sicarios*, teenage assassins who will kill a policeman for anything between $100 and $4000. In the long term, the people of Medellin, home of Colombia's narco-elite, believe that only the legalisation of cocaine in the consuming countries will curb the trade, an argument that is likely to receive short shrift from Western governments.

In the meantime the violence, greed, riches and fear continue to mount, particularly in Colombia, but also anywhere where vast sections of these otherwise bankrupt countries base their survival on the coca leaf and its derivatives. The governments of Colombia, Peru and Bolivia rightly say that the solution is an international one, but until demand recedes the coca production will go on, jeopardizing the prospects of foreign investment and destroying the more benign industry of tourism.

FOOD AND WINE OF THE ANDES

The food and wine of the Andes are distinct from the cuisine of the rest of South America. I do not count 'international food' since no one who wishes to travel would touch the stuff, and in any event it is nothing to do with the Andes. Andean food is basic, it is the food of the simple *campesino*. One might well travel to the Alps for a gastronomic holiday, but not to the Andes. Food is only part of the attraction.

Most restaurants serve a set lunch menu called *almuerzo*. *Desayuno* is breakfast and *cena* supper. South American cuisine reflects the racial heritage of its people – part indigenous Indian and part colonial Spanish. The tomato and the potato were not known in Europe until the Spanish brought them home from the New World. They are a standard accompaniment to most main courses along with local vegetables and the main staples. In Argentina, Venezuela and Colombia this is meat, with a greater emphasis on seafood in Chile and Peru. The sea is never far away from the Andes

---

Milk products are scarce in the Andean regions, as is really good fruit, much of which is diseased, despite external appearances. Fruit and vegetables should always be peeled, cooked or washed in sterilized water. When good fruit can be obtained, it is delicious. Papayas, mangoes, *guanabanas* (custard apple), *lucuna* (egg fruit). *Dulce de membrillo* (quince dessert) and *pasta de guayaba* (guava paste) are popular, often eaten with white cheese as a savoury counterbalance to the sweetness of the fruit.

Venezuela

The distinctive and delicate flavour of many popular local dishes is obtained from the widespread use of local roots and vegetables – such as yucca, yam, sweet potato, *ocumo* and *apio*. *Purée de Apio* is one of the more exotic local roots. When boiled and puréed with salt and butter it tastes like chestnuts. *Tequeños* are a popular starter (thin dough wrapped around a finger of local white cheese and fried until crisp). Beef or chicken hallaca, wrapped in banana leaves and steamed, is another favourite. Also widely available are *empanadas* – turnovers filled with cheese or meat and vegetables.

Beef is prominent on the Venezuelan menu, as *lomito* or *parilla*. A popular substitute for bread is *arepa*, which is a primitive ground cornflour roll, crisp on the outside, soft on the inside. It is sometimes served as a *tostada* filled with meat and vegetables. Cooked bananas and black beans are everyday favourites. *Hervido* is a vegetable, chicken, beef or root soup, while *sancocho* is a ragout of meat and vegetables, especially carrot, corn, pumpkin and marrow (squash) or plantain. Another speciality is *mondongo* (tripe and vegetables).

The Venezuelan sweet tooth is fond of *poche crema* (egg nog), and *bien me sabe* (coconut custard on cake topped with meringue). There are no good wines, but some good beers and rums are made locally. Evening meals are eaten late – from 9 to 11 pm.

Colombia

Despite the wide availability of fish, Colombians tend to prefer meat or chicken. *Ajiaco* is a delicious Bogoteño soup of chicken, potato, maize and cream. *Arroz con pollo* is standard fare on most menus, while a spicier dish (meat, potatoes and chilli) is called *piquete*. *Cuchuco* (meat soup with barley and pepper) and *mazzamorra* (meat and ground maize) are tasty broths. *Arepas*, as in Venezuela, are eaten daily as bread. From Medellin comes the *bendejo paisa*, an elaborate dish of beans, yucca, fried bananas and pork crackling.

Colombian coffee is world famous. It is generally served black, strong and sugared, in a small cup. Ask for a *café* and you will get instant coffee, a *tinto* guarantees the real thing. The local brew, *aguardiente*, is strong and unrefined, as is the local rum, the best makes being *Buc, Viejo de Caldas, Medellín, Añejo* and *Cundinamarca*. Some local wines, of mixed reputation, are available in Colombia. *Santo Tomás* is a full-bodied red wine, while *Vino Moriles* is a Chianti-like wine made under a Domecq patent.

Ecuador

The national drink is the non-alcoholic *naranjillo* (tomato juice that tastes like orange and peach). The local rum, *aguardiente*, is mixed with lemon to form a *paice*. *Locro* is a corn and potato soup, sometimes served with avocado. *Cebiche* (marinated sea food) is common here, as in Peru, while another speciality is *Ilapingachos*, mashed potatoes and cheese with egg. *Humitas* are similar to Mexican *tamales*, a sweetcorn cake. Less palatable to those who keep them as pets at home will be *cuy* or guinea pig, which are widely bred and eaten roasted in Andean regions. Evening meals are eaten about 7.30 pm.

Peru

There are 80 local varieties of Peruvian potato, mostly exported and rarely seen on Peruvian menus, and the Andean Indians have more potato recipes than any other nation. Peruvian *cebiche* is famous and much imitated in neighbouring countries – fish soaked in spicy marinade. *Antichuchos* (marinated sweetbreads) are also popular. The cuisine of the Chiclayo region is acknowledged as the best in the country. Anything prepared *a la Chiclaya* can be recommended. One of the finest sauces, often served with meat or potatoes is *Huancaina*, from the mountain region of the same name. It is made with eggs and cheese. Any dish *a lo macho* comes with shellfish sauce.

Trout is usually good, in Lima or the mountains. Almost every menu offers *lomo saltado*, morsels of beef served with fried potatoes and rice. Guinea pig (*cuy*) is a mountain speciality, served plain, roasted or with peanut sauce. *Pachamanca* (not to be confused with Pachamama, Mother Earth), consists of meat and vegetables cooked in an earth oven over hot stones. Peruvian fast food comes in the form of *anticuchos* (shishkebab of marinated beef heart); *choclo* (corn on the cob) and *picarones* (deep fried calabash batter and molasses.

Desserts are sweet, even by European standards. *Suspiro à la Limeña* is made from sweetened condensed milk and lemon. Other favourites are *Lucuma* (a small brown nutty flavoured fruit) and *chirimoya* (custard apple). Finally, *mazamorra morada* is a sweet made from purple maize, not to be confused with the Colombian savoury dish of the same name.

Pisco sours are a favourite cocktail. This native grape brandy is mixed with lemon, sugar, egg white and nutmeg. *Pisco* is also used in the popular *chilcanos* (with ginger ale) and *algarrobinas* (with carob syrup). The best local beers are *Cusqueña* and *Arequipena*, both forms of stout. There are also brands of Peruvian wine, from the Ica region – *Ocucaje, Tacama* and *El Marqués* are the best. Other Peruvian drinks are *chicha*, which has both alcoholic and non-alcoholic varieties. The teetotallers' version is called *chicha morada* (purple *chicha*), made from maize. Other *chichas* are home brews made from sugar cane. Do not confuse the locally made *Inca Kola* with the international versions of cola – it claims to be the national flavour of Peru and certainly resembles nothing you are likely to have tasted before.

Bolivia

Authentic Bolivian cuisine is mostly found in private houses rather than hotels. Bolivia's marine cuisine was lost with her sea coast in the War of the Pacific, so most modern dishes are based on chicken or beef. From Lake Titicaca, fish (*trucha* – pink salmon trout and *pejerrey*) are plentiful, as are giant frog's legs, many of which are exported to France. Corn, potatoes and *quinoa*, a high protein grain, are grown in the Andes.

A favourite meal, often eaten mid morning at celebrations, is *empanada salteña*, a stew of beef, peas, potatoes, hard-boiled eggs and olives, steeped in a spicy sauce and wrapped in dough. *Picante de pollo* is chicken cooked in *aji* – a very strong chilli. In La Paz, try *plato paceño*, the 'La Paz plate', consisting of corn, potatoes, beans and cheese, well suited to a *marraquetta* bread accompaniment. Poorer *campesinos* eat a lot of mutton, goat and llama. Pork is only eaten on special occasions. Soups are a favourite too. Cream soup is made from peanuts, chick peas, cabbage, potatoes and peas; yellow potato soup or *quinoa* soup, made from the grain are eaten in the highlands. Milk products are hard to find, but goat's milk cheese from the Altiplano can be quite good, if a little salty. Another Andean delicacy is the prickly pear (*tuna*) cactus fruit.

Everyday drinks, some with medicinal side effects, include *mate de coca, mate de manzanillo* (camomile tea), and the ever present *chicha*, of dubious ingredients, sold on the street wherever you see a white flag. Take care, especially at the higher altitudes of the Altiplano – it is easy to have one too many when sampling the local brew. Bolivian beer will appeal to most Europeans, based as it is on German brewing methods. Some local wines are made in the south, and Bolivia has its own version of *pisco – singani* – which is distilled from grapes.

Chile

Empanadas head the average Chilean menu – pastry turnovers baked with onions, eggs, raisins, olives, spices, meat or fish – served as a starter with red wine. *Empanadas de horno* are the size of a large Cornish pasty, a dough filled with ground meat, chopped onion, hard-boiled egg, olives and raisins and then baked. Many meals are accompanied by *chanco de piedra*, a piquant sauce for meat, made by grinding tomatoes, onions, garlic and spices in a stone mortar. *Humitas* are made from the season's tender first corn, freshly ground with onion and peppers, wrapped in corn leaves and boiled for an hour. *Pastel de choclo* is a mixture of *empanadas* and *humitas* – a corn pie. *Porotos granados* contains freshly picked beans cooked with ground corn, squash, sweet basil and other spices.

Very much a people's dish is *cazuela de ave*, a broth served after the *empanada* and consisting of carrots, pumpkin, herbs, chicken and beans. *Bife à la pobre* is a gaucho's lunch; a big steak with fried potatoes, onions and fried eggs. Meat *a la parrillada* is often served on an individual charcoal grill for each table. Apart from recognized cuts of beef, you can expect to be served almost any part of a cow's anatomy. Braised beef (*churrasco*) may be a safer bet for the squeamish. From Easter Island and Chiloé comes the *curanto*. You will not find this in a city restaurant, since the authentic *curanto* is cooked in a hole in the ground on hot stones. The food – peas, pork, seafood and almost anything handy – is wrapped in wet sacks, and takes some hours to cook, making for an unusual outdoor feast.

Chile has the world's longest sea coast – some 6,000 km (4,000 miles) and so fresh fish and seafood are abundant. *Chupe de marisco* (seafood stew) is popular. A staple fish is the *corvina* (sea bass), but more unusual fare is available in the form of *caldillo de congrio* (conger eel soup) and *erizos* (sea urchin).

Chile produces the best wines of South America, good enough to be imported to the US, France and the UK. The reputation of Chilean wines has suffered recently as a result of the Sorbitol additive scandal. The test of a good wine-making country is not just the best wines, but the depth of quality throughout the price range – and the everyday Chilean table wines are excellent value. Red and white are equally good, Concha y Toro, Undurraga and Macul are among the best labels.

The Chilean grape also produces three other national drinks, *Pisco* brandy, *chicha* and *aguardiente*. The latter is claimed to be the root of the Chilean phrase for teatime – *Las Once*. Literally this translates as 'elevenses', but is believed to hark back to the men slipping out of genteel afternoon tea parties to the kitchen for a shot of the real stuff – *aguardiente* – which has eleven letters. So Chilean teatime is now known – in the vernacular – as *Las Once*.

Argentina

The Argentinian cuisine centres on meat, with every variety of grill, roast, blood pudding, hamburger and *milanesa* on offer. Meat is the food of the pampas, more than of the mountains, but is available everywhere. Almost all meat dishes are served with potatoes or chips, making the 'steak and chips mentality' of the Argentine table the least foreign of the South American continent. Chicken, lamb and pork are also much in evidence, baked, roasted or in stews (*pucheros*).

Yerba maté, a bitter herb tea, is the national drink of Argentina, but the country produces some good wines too. Tipped to become a popular wine in the next few decades in Europe is Malbec, from the Mendoza region. San Telmo Malbec and Trapiche are both reliably good, as well as Lopez, Norton, Esmeralda and Weinert.

1 *Pisaq market, Peru.*

2 *Pisaq market, Peru.*

3 *Quito, Ecuador. Tom Conti tops the bill beneath a colonial skyline.*

4 *Macchu Picchu, Peru.*

5   Terraces seen from Inca pathways above Pisaq.

6   Intihuatana, near Pisaq, Peru.

7 *Chimborazo, Ecuador. 6310m (20,703ft).*

8 *Chuquiraguas, seen at around 4000m
(13,000ft).*

9 *Cordillera Urubamba from the Izcuchaca*
   road, near Cuzco, Peru.

10 *The road to Riobamba, Ecuador, with El Altar.*

11 *Spanish colonial spine of the Archbishop's palace, Quito, Ecuador.*

12 *Cordillera Urubamba from the high plains of Chinchero, near Cuzco, Peru.*

CHAPTER 6 Visiting the Andes

London is the European centre for discounted flights from so-called 'bucket shops'. Flight seasons and pricing vary from airline to airline. Low season is roughly September to June, and high season is July and August. The main European holiday times coincide with the normally drier Andean winter. For more detailed weather patterns see below. Bogota, Lima and Quito are the main airports for the northern and central Andes, with flights from London often being routed via Miami or Caracas. Santiago de Chile is a convenient starting point for the southern Andes, with flights routed via Rio de Janeiro.

Whatever flight arrangements you make, be sure that you are fully aware of any restrictions on change of dates, etc., since the cheaper airlines will very likely insist on following the ticket to the letter, even if they have not fulfilled their side of the bargain.

In the cheaper bracket, Viasa are generally thought to be more reliable than Avianca, but you may think that travelling with a European airline is a better investment. Otherwise your South American adventure may start earlier than you thought – with a long delay at Gatwick. My most recent South American adventure did indeed start in Gatwick and ended, three weeks later, at 2 am in Heathrow. Having taken 72 hours on the outward journey, Avianca did not even miss the chance to dump me at the wrong airport. Paying for a slightly more expensive ticket will at least give you rather more peace of mind on the outward journey, as well as the feeling that your ticket will be honoured when the rumour of yet another coup flashes round the backstreets of La Paz.

THE 'GRINGO TRAIL'

You can expect to meet travellers from all walks of life and of all ages on a South American trip. Most visited are the central Andes of Ecuador, Peru and Bolivia. The most well-trodden centres of tourist interest within them are linked by an invisible line so neatly captured by Jack Kerouac's phrase 'the gringo trail'. 'Gringo' is a word used in all the Latin American countries, denoting foreigner, often in a derogatory sense. It may originate from the word for a Greek ('Griego') or more likely from the much-used insult for US soldiers in green uniforms ('Green-go-home').

South America attracts all types, from the student backpacker to the better off adventure seeker to the older tourist who has seen everything else. There are really no limitations, except to bear in mind that South American travel can be quite arduous for the very old and for the very young. Also the scarcity of milk products and the rudimentary nature of food hygiene may not suit very young children. South America is a long-haul destination in many senses. Although the Andean countries seem far away, once you have arrived your money travels far.

Travellers are split loosely into two types –

those on holiday and those 'on the road'. Holidaymakers will have less time on their hands, will want to make advance reservations and often will want to visit a number of destinations in a short time, necessitating taxi rides, internal flights and an altogether more expensive way of travel.

In South America, as elsewhere, time is money. If you have a lot of time on your hands, once you have arrived you can live and travel very cheaply – £7 or $10 per day would be quite feasible. Travellers on the road tend to travel with just a backpack (*mochileros*), following the seasons and the lie of the land, taking local buses and trains or hitch-hiking. It is always possible for the solitary traveller to join others for a period along the gringo trail. The traveller in South America is rarely alone.

There is no doubt that to travel at ground level on local buses and trains without schedules and deadlines is the best way to see the real South America, but it takes time and nerve. An organized trip will at least cover the ground and get you to where you want to go in a given time period. There are advantages in both styles of travel.

WEATHER AND WHEN TO GO

There is no single weather pattern in the Andes, particularly when you recollect that the range is some 6000 km (4000 miles) from north to south. What one can say in general terms is that the seasons are the opposite of those in the northern hemisphere, so June is the month of the Winter Solstice and their July is like our January. Although you would be correct in assuming from this that the Chilean and Argentinian skiing seasons are the opposite of ours, it would be wrong to draw more detailed conclusions. What is more useful to know is whether it will be clear or cloudy, wet or dry. In the Andes the intermediate seasons of spring and autumn do not really exist. It is either the wet season or dry season.

The Andes can be visited all year round, but November to February are the wettest, making trekking and outdoor excursions difficult and marring the views. In the 'winter' (May to September) the weather is cooler and clearer, a better time all round for a visit. The same applies to the northern and central parts of Chile and Argentina, which can be visited at any time. Further south, winter grips from April to September. September to March are therefore best for the southern Andes.

Andean weather from north to south

Venezuela's climate is tropical, with little change from season to season. Temperature differences are mainly a function of altitude. At any time of year it tends to be warm around midday. The driest time of year is from December to April.

Colombia is the true beginning of the northern Andes, with the climate being affected by Caribbean and Pacific trade winds. Bogota has a climate equivalent to the European spring or summer for most of the year. December to February are the driest months, but are also the months when many locals take their holidays. The Colombian Andes are somewhat lower than they are to the south. June to September can be very wet in most areas. Others will tell you that the rainy periods are March/April and October/November – so rain gear is advised for all visits!

The mountains, people and climate of **Ecuador** are less harsh than those of her neighbour Peru to the south, but the weather is unpredictable. The capital, Quito, with a mean temperature of 59°F (15°C), seems springlike for most of the year, but can be cold in the

34. *The road to Riobamba.* Collectivo *bus beneath El Altar massif, Ecuador.*

evenings. The climate is reliably unreliable. The coast is affected greatly by the December *El Niño* current, while inland to the east, the *oriente* jungle region is almost always wet. In the middle, the eastern Ecuadorian Andes are influenced by jungle weather, the wettest months being June to August. December to January are often the best for clear weather and successful ascents of the main eastern peaks. In the western Ecuadorian Andes, dry weather prevails from late July to September, while February to May are wet, April being the wettest month.

The **Peruvian Andes** are dry and temperate between April and November, being driest in June and July. The Andes here are more influenced by Pacific winds. From mid-November to March is the rainy season. Peru has arguably the most spectacular mountains and Inca festivals, both of which are at their best in July–September, when the crowds of European tourists are at their worst. Transport, accommodation and good manners are at their hardest to find during this period.

The **Bolivian Andes** and **Altiplano** have a dry season that runs approximately from May to November, with a daytime average of 60°F (16°C). From June to August (winter) night temperatures can be cold. November to March is the rainy season, often flooding the Altiplano and shrouding the capital, La Paz, in fog.

In **Argentina**, the ski resort of Bariloche is almost Alpine with swimming in summer and skiing in winter, while the high Andes are often dry and temperate.

Chile is a country of extremes. The Atacama Desert is one of the driest and hottest places on Earth, but will still freeze at night. The Chilean Lake District has a temperate Mediterranean climate but it is frequently chilled by mountain winds. The high passes are blocked by winter snow and the ski pistes can be covered from May to October. Southern Chile is mostly cold and extremely windy.

Ideally, if you have the luxury or being able to plan your visit, it would be best to avoid the rainy season, the peak tourist seasons, particularly if you plan to hike or climb – when the weather will have maximum effect on the pleasure, even the safety, of your visit. There is much to be said for a visit at the 'wrong time of year'. The weather can always pleasantly surprise you, and even if the mountains are frequently obscured, there are still the people, the fiestas and the music of the Andes.

The weather can always turn dangerously bad at any time of year in the mountains, and it is wise to be well prepared. Walkers run into difficulties in the hills of England in high summer, let alone the Andes. Remember that the Andes are the second-highest mountain range in the world, and plan accordingly.

INSURANCE

Comprehensive travel insurance is recommended, to include loss of baggage, personal effects and delay/cancellation. Be sure to have full winter sports coverage and mountaineering extensions since the cost of a mountain rescue, assuming it is available, can run into thousands of pounds or dollars. Check that the small print includes emergency repatriation. Many companies sell good general travel insurance. For mountaineering I have found that the British Mountaineering Council's annual policy is excellent value.

MONEY

The only form of foreign currency that is useful, indeed essential, in South America, is the US dollar. Your pockets may bulge with Deutschmarks or pounds sterling, but you could still starve. Dollars are standard currency. Travel-

35. Peru, the open road near Chinchero. The land which campesinos leave behind in their migration to cardboard ghettos in the cities.

ler's cheques should also be purchased in US dollars, preferably from a major international supplier. American Express has offices in many South American cities, where cheques can be cashed, lost or stolen cheques refunded, mail forwarded and travel services obtained. It is also worth carrying some cash dollars in small denominations for small, out of hours transactions. Almost all South American currencies are worthless outside the country of origin or its immediate neighbour and are best kept as souvenirs! Change only what you need or convert any excess back to dollars before leaving the country.

Many hotels, American Express offices, government banks and official *cambios* will change traveller's cheques and cash at the official rate. In most cases the black market operates in the street, a few footsteps from the bank door. Exchange rates are generally better than the official rate, sometimes two or three times as much. However, there are a number of disadvantages. First, although the black market is widely tolerated, it is illegal, and the degree of enforcement varies from day to day. One day a policeman might watch a black market transaction with a friendly smile, the next day you might be arrested. Also, you might be given forged notes, or short changed, or have your money snatched. The risks are always there and must be left to the individual traveller to assess.

I have met travellers who have been on the road for some months or even a year, have never changed money at a bank, and who have effectively doubled their money during their travels. Others prefer the safe but more costly method of official exchange. It should be added that for someone earning American or European salaries prices in the Andes are cheap and your money goes a long way whatever exchange rate is obtained. Be sure to hide your money before

leaving the bank and walking onto the street. Thieves know you will be loaded with cash.

DOCUMENTS AND SECURITY

Identity documents (passports or identity card) should be carried at all times. You should carry separately a photocopy of all the main documents; passport title page, birth certificate, insurance documents, traveller's cheques receipts and refund instructions, airline tickets, reservation confirmations, etc. In the event of a theft or loss you will then have some chance of picking up the pieces of your journey. Spread your valuables widely about your person or give copies to a travelling companion. Moneybelts, secret pockets, stashes under the insoles of your shoes – all of these serve the purpose and spread the risk.

ANDEAN TIME

Caracas (Venezuela) and La Paz (Bolivia) are four hours behind GMT, while the other Andean capitals (Bogotá, Lima, Quito, Santiago) are five hours behind GMT. Andean time is therefore almost on a par with the east coast of the USA. As far as local appointments are concerned, interpretation of time is very flexible. Locals do not consider it rude to be an hour late for an appointment, but a rather quaint agreement to meet *a la hora ingelsa* (English time) means that at least they will try and be on time. Likewise, most estimates of time for journeys, distances, etc. are likely to be wildly inaccurate, and are often two or three times more than stated.

THE ANDES BY CAR – THE LAWLESS ROADS

With hand on heart I could not recommend the car as a way to travel in the Andes. Driving is frantic in the cities, traffic laws are rarely obeyed. In the mountains, road conditions are

36. On the road in Peru – travelling by truck is the norm for country roads.

71

terrible, signposts few, police, telephones and road assistance practically non-existent. Outside the cities, anything less than a four-wheel drive vehicle would be unwise. Car hire is surprisingly expensive even by first world standards, while maintenance standards are decidedly third world.

Andean roads are a jarring morale-breaking adventure into heat, dust, cold and delay. In cities do not trust lights or traffic signals. No one else obeys them. Treat cities or villages like a visit to a safari park – remove detachable accessories and hide them with your valuables out of sight in the boot. Mountain travel in the rainy season is almost impossible, with frequent snow, landslides and rockfalls blocking roads or washing them away. They may stay closed until the dry season. The high altitude requires spark plugs and carburettor jets to be specially adjusted, while there is little chance of mechanical assistance or police patrols. Highway robbery with improvised road blocks is not unknown. Aim to be self-sufficient in food, water, fuel and spares for long distances.

37. The road to Riobamba, beneath El Altar massif.

If you really must take a particular route that is not serviced by bus or train, consider hitchhiking (although not always very safe) by truck, since private cars are rare. Expect to pay the driver. Even for quite long journeys, hiring a taxi can work out considerably cheaper and less stressful than hiring a car. If you cannot resist the lure of high altitude trucking, join an organized truck trip with overland experts such as Exodus or Encounter Overland.

Bus, train and truck are the cheap local way to travel. Schedules are rarely observed, breakdowns and delays are frequent. For those with time on their hands and who want to see the Andes through the eyes of a *campesino* this is the way to travel. Bear in mind that road journeys can seem to last an eternity.

INTERNAL FLIGHTS

If time is a problem, an internal flight may be the answer. Book well ahead for peak destinations such as Cuzco. Reconfirm all bookings. Double booking is a common practice, so turn up well in advance to claim your seat. The main South American airlines offer internal flight packages, which may save time and indeed money for the traveller in a hurry. Enquire through the tourist offices at home well in advance of departure. Some packages are only available if purchased in your country of origin.

WHAT TO TAKE

What to take depends very much on what style of travel you have adopted – organized tour or *mochilero*, and whether you intend to camp or stay in hotels. Whatever your choice, keep everything to a minimum. Do not expect to obtain good quality hiking or camping equipment along the way – although in some of the main mountaineering centres equipment of questionable quality can be obtained. Good quality lightweight walking boots are essential, as is good quality rain gear, preferably breathable, such as Gore-Tex. A number of thin layers of warm clothing are more useful than one heavy jacket.

Because Andean weather changes hourly, you will need spare clothing with you most of the day, so a small day pack is an essential for this as well as your camera, maps and snacks. A thermos/unbreakable water bottle is very useful since the high altitudes are very dehydrating and a warm drink can do wonders for morale when the sun dips behind a cloud and a cold wind blasts off the Altiplano. If your clothing and luggage look unenviably humble, then so much the better. This will minimize the chances of your becoming a target for thieves. Jewellery and expensive watches should be left at home.

They may also be hedged around with restrictions, so read the small print carefully and follow procedural regulations to the letter on arrival.

HEALTH

Public health standards in South America are improving steadily. Many endemic diseases have been contained or eradicated. The adventurous Andean traveller will be exposed to a number of hazards, but these can mostly be avoided by advance planning and sensible conduct on the way.

Few Andean countries have any mandatory regulations prior to entry, so the majority of precautions are self-imposed common sense. Visitors who are at greatest risk are those visiting the Andes for a short time. Many health problems are associated with dietary change and lower standards of food hygiene. It should be noted, however, that South American visitors to North America, where food standards are high, have also been known to suffer from the 'Inca's revenge', so the greatest problem is not just poorer standards, but a change of microbes.

In particular, if you are going to South America to see the Andes, you will fly perhaps from sea level to Andean airports between 2,500–4000 m (8000–13,000 ft) up. On arrival at these altitudes after a 12 to 18 hour flight, lack of acclimatization is a problem that, if not addressed immediately, can cost a few vital days of the trip. You will also start the trip tired and sick from altitude and thus more prone to catching whatever is around. The long-haul traveller has the luxury of taking his time to settle into the altitude and become used to the food. He will generally stay the course better than the short-term traveller.

This does not purport to be a technical summary, but a layman's guide to good health in the Andes. The first step should be a visit, well ahead of time, to your local doctor, or ideally a tropical medicine centre, such as the

St Pancras Hospital for Tropical Diseases, or the British Airways Medical Centre (75 Regent Street, London W1, tel: 071 439 9584). They will give the necessary advice and injections. Do go well ahead of time since some inoculations require boosters before travel.

The main recommended inoculations for the Andes are those against typhoid, cholera, yellow fever, polio, tetanus, and gamma globulin (against hepatitis). Hepatitis A (jaundice) is commonly caught through poor food hygiene. The more serious hepatitis B can be caught through sexual contact, infected needles, etc. The normal precautions taken against Aids will cover hepatitis. Particular advice may be required for small children, since many of the infections they are prone to are more serious in South America. The chances of contracting something are higher, while medical care is poorer and harder to obtain.

Rabies

Rabies is a risk in the Andes. A form of inoculation can be had in advance, the main benefit of which is to give you more time to get treatment after receiving a rabid bite. On the road, avoid dogs and cats, cover yourself at night – vampire bats do exist! If bitten try and detain the offending animal and have it examined by a local hospital to see if you need a course of treatment. This is the only conclusive method of determining whether the animal is rabid. The alternative is to assume rabies and begin treatment.

Malaria

Malaria is endemic in most of South America, but the female of the malarial mosquito (which carries the disease) does not inhabit altitudes in excess of 2500 m (8000 ft). Therefore, most of the Andes are safe. However, even a stopover at lower altitude is enough to receive a malarial bite so the safe approach is to take the recommended malarial prophylactics for the stopover destination. Most courses start a week before travel and continue six weeks after to cover the incubation period. The follow up course is often neglected but it is dangerous to do so. Malaria can go undiagnosed on return home and this is how most modern fatalities occur from an otherwise treatable disease. Even taking all precautions it is sometimes still possible to contract malaria – the parasite has developed immunity to some of the latest drugs, and the chemists are only just keeping ahead.

Snakes

Snakes are widely distributed, particularly in montane forest regions such as on the Inca trail – many are extremely venomous. It is rare for someone to die of snakebite, the more likely cause of death is from shock or fright. In most cases only a fraction of the full venom is delivered by the snake, because clothing, footwear, etc. prevent full penetration of the fangs. Snakebite kits can be carried, but they are usually specific for a particular snake venom. The proper treatment in the form of the actual antidote for the particular type of snake can only effectively be administered by a doctor.

Prevention is, as usual, better than cure. The vast majority of snakes will avoid human contact and are as frightened of us as we are of them. Swishing the grass with a stick and making plenty of noise will scare most snakes away. Strong boots, even snake boots, for jungle regions offer maximum protection up to knee level. Thick trousers are a help too. If someone is bitten, a tourniquet, released for 90 seconds every 15 minutes, should be applied to the limb. The victim should be reassured, kept calm and taken to a hospital. If the offending snake can be killed and brought to the hospital this will speed antidote selection.

Food hygiene

Ideally, only drink bottled mineral water or sterilized water – various pills and kits are available, or local iodine can be used. Avoid salads washed in unsterilized water, avoid ice for the same reasons. Although food from market stalls is cheap and looks appetizing, it is usually prepared with poor hygiene and is best avoided. Safest are well-cooked soups or stews. If you suffer stomach upsets, be sure to take in plenty of liquids, since dehydration is a double danger at altitude. Most attacks should pass within three days. If not, or if there is blood in your stools, a doctor should be consulted. It is worth carrying an antidiarrhoeal such as Lomotil to tide you over until normal eating can be resumed. About 4000 calories per day is recommended for trekkers, 5000 for climbers.

MOUNTAIN DANGERS

Altitude

Altitude-related problems in the Andes should be seen against the context of what we think is high in the European Alps. In the Alps the majority of problems occur in the 2500 m to 5000 m range (8000 to 16,000 ft). Cable cars make such altitudes easily accessible. Mont Blanc, the highest summit in the Alps, is 4807 m (15,771 ft). Mechanical transport in the Alps will take you to the top of the Jungfraujoch (3454 m – 11,332 ft) and the Aiguille du Midi téléférique (3842 m – 12,605 ft). Many Alpine villages are in the 1000 m–2000 m (3300 ft to 6500 ft) range.

In the Andes, the destination airport may be anywhere between 2500 m (8000 ft) and 4000 m (13,000 ft) above sea level. In South America, some seven million people live permanently between 3650 m (12,000 ft) and 4250 m (14,000 ft). Except in the few ski resorts, cable cars are non-existent, and access to such alti-tudes is by road and rail. Freezing temperatures may be encountered at any time of the year at this altitude. Some Andean mining villages exist at 5340 m (17,500 ft) but attempts to establish permanent settlements at even higher altitudes have failed because of altitude sickness. It would appear that the human body is not designed for permanent living above these altitudes. Deterioration, not acclimatization, is the pattern above about 4500 m (15,000 ft). Altitude-related problems are a factor of everyday life for normal people in the Andes, let alone mountaineers.

Some of the altitudes encountered by the average tourist on the gringo trail are as follows: roads can take you to as high as 5200 m (17,000 ft – Chacaltaya ski resort in Bolivia), rail to 4830 m (15,846 ft – Volcan mine, Peru) while even capital cities are lofty by European standards – Bogotá 2650 m (8700 ft); Quito 2850 m (9350 ft); La Paz 3636 m (11,900 ft – the highest capital in the world). Other main attractions such as Cuzco (3310 m – 10,800 ft) and Macchu Picchu (2280 m – 7500 ft) are at significant altitudes. The highest pass on the Inca trail is 4200 m (13,800 ft), while Lake Titicaca is at 3800 m (12,500 ft). Treks in Peru's Cordillera Blanca cross high passes of 4500 m (15,000 ft).

Ten days will bring a real improvement in coping with altitude. Maximum acclimatization occurs after about three weeks, probably longer than your holiday. The mountaineers' motto 'climb high, sleep low' is hard to apply in the Andes, since you are always at high altitude, even in the valleys and on the Altiplano, itself at 3650–3900 m (12–13,000 ft).

Against the modest altitude of the Alps, it can be seen that in the Andes altitude presents a real problem for tourists. It is essential to rest for a few days after arrival. Drink plenty of liquids, especially coca tea where available. Eat lightly and avoid excessive use of stimulants such as coffee, or depressants such as alcohol. Altitude sickness takes many forms. Mild attacks include breathlessness, dry throat, loss of appetite, tight chest, inability to sleep, a feeling of lassitude. These symptoms should pass in a few days.

More serious is acute mountain sickness (*soroche*), when fluid collects in the lungs or brain, eventually causing cerebral or pulmonary oedemas. These can be fatal. In most cases relief is immediate on descending to lower altitudes. Coca tea or chewing coca leaves may help as may certain drugs. Diamox, available on prescription in the UK, can sometimes alleviate the problem of water retention by the unacclimatized.

People differ vastly in their ability to adapt to altitude. Strangely, acclimatization bears no relation to fitness. Indeed there is evidence that endurance-trained people, such as marathon runners, are actually less well able to acclimatize to altitude than others. Teenagers may have more problems than mature adults, but there is no evidence that travellers of pensionable age have special altitude problems. Sudden ascents to above 3500 m (11,500 ft) for the unacclimatized can be serious. Anyone suffering badly from altitude should descend for immediate relief. The best precaution is to allow plenty of time to achieve your mountaineering, trekking or travelling objectives. With acclimatization they will be all the more enjoyable. Without it, even modest peaks may be out of reach.

The wind chill factor

When the wind blows in the mountains it changes the face of mother nature. At altitude, there is almost never a snowfall without wind. The winds are funnelled by valleys, passes and natural features. Wind from any direction is a danger signal in the high mountains – it is the builder of avalanches and cornices as well as causing wind chill to poorly protected skin. Cornices are formed by the wind. They resemble a frozen wave crest on the top of ridges, leaning out over the ridge in the leeward direction. The only thing that holds them in place is the tension in the wind-packed snow. The longer they stand, the more dangerous they become.

The effects of wind chill can be moderated by wearing sensible clothing. Some sample figures are shown in the chart below.

So when you are in the eye of the wind, remember the implications: increased avalanche danger, cornice formation, and the wind chill factor.

Hypothermia

Skiers, climbers and walkers who are inadequately dressed and are exposed to cold, wet or wind for sustained periods can quickly become victims of hypothermia. For years mountain hypothermia has been loosely known as exposure, but exposure to the elements is only part of the story. Exposure causes rapid heat loss from the body, leading to a progressive fall in body temperature. Particularly dangerous is the combination of this factor with fatigue, cold, anxiety and mental stress.

The body can be kept warm by layers of still air next to the skin and between garments. When clothes become wet because of bad insulation or

	Wind speed	8 kph (5 mph)	30 kph (20 mph)	50 kph (30 mph)	80 kph (50 mph)
Air temp (°C) 0	Wind chill	−4	−14	−18	−20
−8		−13	−25	−31	−33
−16		−22	−37	−43	−46
−24		−31	−48	−56	−59

excessive sweating, water replaces the layer of air, reducing protection by up to 90 per cent. When this is exacerbated by windy conditions, evaporation takes place resulting in even greater cooling of the body. Once the core temperature of the body falls 6°C or more below normal, the body starts to shiver in an attempt to create heat by involuntary muscular activity.

Prevention of any mountain hazard is obviously better than cure. Proper mountain clothing is the first line of defence, i.e. clothing that keeps you warm in wet or windy conditions. In addition, sensible planning of the route according to the experience, fitness and ability of the party will keep morale high and danger to a minimum. The great danger of hypothermia is that it can be hard to spot. Some of the symptoms include apathy, pallor, disinterest, slow thinking, and inability to perform simple tasks normally well within the capability of the person concerned. Unexpected behaviour is another indication – unreasonable violent outbursts, slurred speech, stumbling, careless footwork, shivering and finally loss of consciousness.

In the mountains, insulation and removal of the causes of hypothermia is the required immediate treatment. Early recognition should be followed by reallocation of loads, a move downhill or downwind, extra clothing, body warming by getting into a huddle, seeking shelter from the wind, warming with hot drinks and energy-giving food. The next step is for the party leader to organize a safe and quick evacuation to a place where a serious case can be actively rewarmed. Remember that once in the grip of hypothermia the sufferer is unable to reason clearly enough to get himself out of trouble. The rest of the party must take this responsibility for him.

Frostbite

Frostbite is, of course, an ever-present risk. It may be purely the result of low temperature, but is more likely to result from a combination of low temperature, wind chill, poor circulation, inadequate clothing, overtiredness, dehydration and hypothermia, among other factors. Care should be taken at all times to give maximum protection to the face, ears, nose, hands and toes. Drink three to four litres of water a day to avoid dehydration.

Snow blindness

Freshly fallen snow reflects up to 90 per cent of sunlight. Solar radiation can be up to four times as strong above 2000 m (6500 ft) than at sea level. Ultraviolet radiation is absorbed by the surface of the eye in the same way as it is absorbed by the skin. The only difference is that the surface of the eye cannot get a tan and develop its own protection. We need to do what nature cannot – and use adequate sunglasses.

Sunburn of the eye tissues results in snow blindness. During the period of exposure only the brightness of the light serves as a warning. Snow blindness develops some eight to ten hours later. Skiers' sunglasses are often seen as just another fashion accessory, but for the off-piste skier and mountaineer who puts in long hours on the snow, light absorbency and side-protection should be the main criteria. Glasses need to absorb over 80 per cent of the light to provide adequate protection. Special mountaineers' glasses (e.g. glacier goggles) are available that fit snugly round the sides of the eye and offer maximum protection.

At really high altitude, goggles may be safer. Do not forget to apply sunscreen to the eyelids to prevent burning. Always carry a spare pair of glasses. In an emergency, lenses can be made out of cardboard with a thin slit to see through – unfashionable, but quite effective. You should not assume that overcast days are any less dangerous – ultraviolet light penetrates just as effectively through cloud.

The first sign of snow blindness is a dry irritation of the eyes, perhaps a flickering in front of the eye followed by a burning sensation and finally a feeling as if the eyes are full of sand. Blinking and exposure to any light source can be extremely painful. Confinement to a darkened room for a few days with cold compresses is often the best remedy for acute cases – punishment indeed for a few hours of carelessness. Happily, in most cases the eyes heal spontaneously and there are no lasting effects.

Other dangers for mountaineers

In addition to the above, there are a number of other mountain dangers, understanding and avoidance of which are beyond the scope of this book. Glaciers present their share of dangers, not least crevasses, while the danger of avalanche is ever present above the snowline, which should be approached with even greater caution than in Europe. In the Andes the chance of an organized rescue party coming to the aid of a mountain emergency is virtually nil; distances are too great, communications too poor, rescue services too fragmented. Therefore all mountaineering trips should be planned on the basis of self-sufficiency.

With so many active volcanoes, it is no surprise that the Andes is an area where earthquakes of varying degrees are often encountered, and these can have a catastrophic effect on whole regions. In 1970 the north face of Huascaran (Peru's highest mountain 6768 m, 22,200 ft) detached itself from the main peak after an earthquake, sending an avalanche of snow, rock and debris 80 km (50 miles) into the valley, destroying the town of Yungay and making thousands homeless.

In 1976, a party of climbers was engulfed in an eruption on the ascent of Sangay (5320 m – 17,454 ft). This peak, one of the world's most active volcanoes, is known to involve Russian roulette-style odds of an eruption on the upper slopes. A British party was caught by an eruption when on the summit ice-field, and were carried down 600 m (2000 ft). Two died and three miraculously survived after a rescue by a separate climbing party.

Obviously the risk of avalanches being spontaneously triggered is far greater in volcano and earthquake terrain than in the geologically less active Alps, but in both ranges the fact remains that avalanche accidents are still most often caused when the climbing/skiing party itself triggers a suspect slope.

SECURITY

Running the Andean gauntlet

'They are so poor. We are so rich'
– Philosophical Swiss tourist at Cuzco's
Macchu Picchu station, after just having
his bag slashed and camera stolen.

In most of the Andes, the average annual earnings of an agricultural worker may be little more than $500, assuming he has a job. With failed harvests, floods and fluctuating produce prices, the flight to the cities has assumed the status of a migration. Remember then that even the poorest gringo traveller may well be carrying the equivalent of a year's salary, especially when you consider the value of film and camera gear. Consequently the traveller presents an attractive target for thieves. Although the vast majority of country people are polite and honest, street crimes – theft and muggings – have become a predictable certainty of most South American trips.

The most dangerous places are those that are very busy or very quiet. Busy confusing places such as markets, bus and train stations and airports are favourite haunts of the thief, who will rely on confusion and distraction to strike. Late at night and early in the morning are particularly dangerous times. Try and avoid arrival or departure late at night and take taxis if you do arrive at these times. Be particularly careful about daypacks as these are known to contain most of the valuables.

Your wallet should contain only what is needed for the day; the rest should be hidden. Camera and bag straps should be reinforced, perhaps with wire to avoid cutting. Where possible leave valuables in a respectable hotel safe. A chain or padlock is useful in trains or buses – luggage frequently vanishes from the roof in transit!

In high risk areas develop a habit of wearing your pack on your front, ideally secured to your belt with an extra strap. A favourite method of attack is for the victim to be jostled and distracted, while his associates slash the bag with a razor and extract the contents. In most cases it is done so skilfully that the victim does not realize what has happened until much later.

The same types of theft are often repeated at the same place, day after day, time after time. More often than not victims have read warnings in the *South American Handbook* or elsewhere and have thought 'it could not happen to me'. Distraction is the usual method: a seemingly innocent conversation, showing a foreign coin, smearing mustard or dirt on your face, jostling when getting in or out of transport, when you are in the lavatory, or even the shower (lock your door and window – or take valuables inside).

Thefts are quite common at the point of exchange in a black market currency transaction. Watch out too for thieves on mopeds. If you do encounter a civil disturbance or some sort of demonstration, avoid it as it may be used as cover for looting and lawlessness even beyond the norm. Another ruse is to engage the traveller in some spurious argument. Tiredness and tension will make your temper all the easier to inflame, and such arguments are often the

distraction that makes a theft possible. More unpleasant examples are drugged sweets or drinks – accept nothing from strangers. While most thefts are by stealth, mugging is on the increase. Walking alone at night or even by day in known poor areas is asking for trouble, especially brandishing a camera.

> The traveller needs to be constantly alert to avoid becoming a victim – the thief will probably select an easier target. Theft avoidance after a while becomes a matter of habit rather than a bore, and although insurance and traveller's cheque refunds can compensate for most things, there will be the inevitable delay in dealing with the bureaucracy before satisfaction is achieved.
>
> Before leaving home, obtain a good insurance package that covers the full length of your stay, and can be extended if necessary. Ensure that you are covered for the full value of your possessions, or the company will apply 'average' in the case of a claim, and obtain full medical cover for at least £100,000 as well as emergency repatriation. If you do have something stolen, make a full *denuncia* at the police station local to the scene of the crime, and obtain a copy of it. This will be necessary for any claim.

Peru currently has the worst reputation for theft from tourists, especially in Cuzco, the Cuzco-Macchu Picchu station, and more recently on the Inca Trail, which is not recommended in groups of less than six. Poorer city areas in Venezuela should be avoided, as they should in Colombia. In Ecuador, Guayaquil needs special caution, as does the Quito old town. Bolivia is generally safe but more incidents are reported every year. Argentina and Chile have a better reputation in the main tourist areas.

Women travelling alone

Modern European attitudes to women travelling alone have not filtered through to the Andes. A woman travelling alone may be assumed to be disreputable in male-dominated societies where family life at home is the norm. A combination of colonial *machismo* and North American television has resulted in the woman alone being regarded as fair game, which at best is psychologically wearing, at worst dangerous. Many of the wolf whistles are harmless, and a protestation of being *casada* (married) may or may not be believed. There are many places, however, where a single woman will be greeted with no more than curiosity and courtesy, so commonsense standards apply. Probably the best bet is to travel in a group, preferably mixed. It is easy to meet fellow travellers along the gringo trail.

Some useful tips for a woman travelling alone are to do a basic language course, look purposeful and have a good idea of where you are going. Ask local women if your destination is considered safe; avoid walking at night and waiting alone at stations. It may be possible to ask a respectable-looking family if you can wait with them. Do not travel too many hours in a day, since your wits will be dulled by tiredness. You will be less likely to spot a difficult situation that a fresher mind might have anticipated. In fact, this advice would apply equally well to any man travelling alone.

Drugs

Despite being the point of origin of much of the world's cocaine, South American countries are hard on anyone suspected of dealing or trafficking in drugs. Human rights and the legal system are not up to American or European standards. An accused person can await trial for years without any form of legal representation. Your own country may be unwilling or unable to intervene in an offence allegedly involving drugs, especially in view of recent Western collaboration aimed at cracking the cocaine trade. Rumours of officials planting cocaine with a view to extorting bribes are too numerous to be completely without foundation. Baggage should always be locked in transit, and should your bags be searched at customs, it is wise to try and arrange for this to be done in front of witnesses.

Terrorism

The activities of terrorists have hit headlines in Peru and Colombia. Much of the northern part of Peru is effectively out of bounds because of guerrilla activity. Although the Sendero Luminoso have not been sufficiently organized to formulate a policy about tourists, they are not above indiscriminate killing of tourists who get in the way, as an incident in Huaras demonstrated in 1989. If you are thought to be an American anti-drugs operator in Colombia, your life will certainly be at risk. The warnings put out by the Foreign Office have a factual basis, and should be adhered to.

In conclusion, if you want a guaranteed safe holiday in the mountains, do not go to the Andes. However, the vast majority of travellers who visit the South American continent come home with magical memories that they would never obtain in the Alps or elsewhere. Indeed the sort of traveller to whom the South American experience appeals is not put off by the odd story of buccaneering along the way. It is all part of the adventure. Travellers who have problems in the Andes tend to have them anywhere in the world, while those who approach the Andes with their eyes and ears open are likely to come home unscathed.

THE VENEZUELAN ANDES AT A GLANCE

General situation

The security situation at Venezuela has deteriorated in recent months, with street crime and car thefts showing a sharp increase. Violence is common. Visitors should exercise appropriate care, avoid wearing expensive jewellery and watches and stay away from risky areas. All visitors, particularly women, are strongly advised not to accept lifts from unmarked taxis, but to go to official taxi ranks. At Caracas International Airport, taxi tickets for the journey into town are available from a special booth at the terminal. (Foreign Office – July 1990).

Capital: Caracas.

Population: 14 million.

Main Andean ranges: Cordillera de Mérida; Sierra Nevada National Park; Sierra de Santa Domingo.

Highest and best known summits: Pico Bolivar 5007 m (16,400 ft); Humboldt and Bonpland 4920 m (16,000 ft); El Toro 4720 m (15,500 ft); Mucuñuque 4720 m (15,300 ft); Mirror Peak (Pico Espejo) 4765 m (15,633 ft), accessible by one of the world's longest 12.5 km (8 miles), and highest cable cars.)

Best known Andean towns/resorts: Mérida; Los Nevados (highest mountain village in Venezuela), trips through Club Andino.

Other features: Numerous mountain lakes on the *paramos*, the largest of which is at Mucubaji 3540 m (11,600 ft); the Orinoco River; ski mountaineering from November to May in the Sierra Nevada National Park at 4270 m (14,000 ft); the *frailejón* (the 'great friar'), a beautiful plant found only on the *paramos*.

Tourist offices: London: Venezuelan Embassy, Consular Section, 56 Grafton Way, London W1P 5LB; Telephone: 071 387 6727.
New York: Venezuelan Consulate, 7 East 51st Street, New York 10022; Telephone: 212 826 1660.

Visa: British passport holders – a 60-day tourist card is issued by authorized airlines. A return ticket and a passport valid for a minimum of six months is required. USA passport holders – as British.

Embassies/Consulates to be contacted in case of tourist difficulty:
British: Edificio Torre Las Mercedes, Piso 3, Ciudad Comercial Tamanaco, P.O. Apartado 1246, Caracas 101A; Telephone: 911255.
USA: Avenida Francisco de Miranda, La Floresta; Telephone: 284 6111.

Languages: The local language is Spanish. English is spoken in some larger resorts.

Currency: Approximate exchange rate, £1.00 = 80 Bolivars (Bs.) Dollars preferred. Gratuities: 10 per cent. Most major credit cards and traveller's cheques accepted. Bank opening times: 8.30 am to 11.30 am; 2.00 pm to 4.30 pm Monday to Friday. Black market – officially none.

Electricity: 110 volts, AC 60 cycles.

Accommodation: Advance reservations are necessary for hotels. Good camping facilities are rare.

Air travel: Most convenient international airport for US and European connections: Aeropuerto International Simón Bolívar. Internal flights are available. Airport departure tax: US$3.50 tourist, US$16 business.

Car travel: Rental self-drive cars are available in major city centres, but are expensive. A British driving licence is accepted, but an International Driving Permit is more useful. Passport and identification should be carried at all times.

Speed limits on roads: 80 kph (50 mph). Car touring club: Touring y Automóvil Club de Venezuela, Locales 11-14, Cetro Integral, 'Santa Rosa de Lima', Caracas, Telephone: 02-915571. Petrol is widely available. Driving is on the right.

Rail travel on Andean routes: the only Andean line is from Mérida to Pico Espejo.

Maps: Best available locally. 1:100,000 Instituto Cartografico, Caracas.

Medical: No inoculations are required, but insurance is advised.

Weather: The best time of year to visit is from November to May, ideally January to April. The temperature in the cold zone (above 2000 m – 6500 ft) averages 16°C (60°F).

Mountaineering club: Club Andino, Universidad de los Andes, Mérida.

THE COLOMBIAN ANDES AT A GLANCE

General situation

Colombian life is violent. The country's history is punctuated by civil wars between Liberals and Conservatives, culminating in the 1950s period of carnage known simply as *la violencia*. The result of this was the carving up of power between two main political parties. The power of regional political barons has increased dramatically and weakened the clout of central authority to deal with the new breed of baron – the *extraditables*.

These barons, whose activities the US and Europe are keen to suppress, are epitomized by drug dealers whose private armies and power have brought the government and the country to their knees. The US has become involved in attempts to curb the production of cocaine centred on Medellín and Cali, Colombia's second and third cities. In September 1989 the British Foreign Office was advising foreigners to stay away from the Medellín area of Colombia, where the drug barons have threatened to kill 'foreigners' on the basis that they might be involved with American-backed anti-cocaine armies. Since this announcement the drug cartels placed a bomb that brought down an Avianca plane, killing 107 people. Elections were disrupted by a campaign of terror. Judges were shot and officials resigned. Free press newspapers were bombed. Meanwhile, police activity has triggered further bombings and the drug war continues.

Capital: Bogota.

Population: 30 million.

Main Andean ranges: With the exception of an independent range known as the Sierra Nevada de Santa Marta, there are three main Andean ranges, the Cordilleras Central (central), Occidental (western) and the Oriental (the largest, eastern, range in which the capital, Bogota, is set.) The Occidental is some 800 km (500 miles) long and rises to 5700 m (18,700 ft).

Highest and best known summits: Sierra Nevada de Santa Marta – Pico Cristobal Colon and Pico Simon Bolivar, both 5775 m (18,950 ft). Cordillera Oriental – Alto Ritacuba 5493 m (18,021 ft). Cordilleras Occidental & Central – Nevado de Huila 5350 m (17,552 ft); Nevado del Ruiz 5320 m (17,453 ft), ski lodge with road access to 4790 m (15,715 ft).

Best known Andean towns/resorts: Nevado del Ruiz is the most developed Andean resort. The volcano is currently active and the authorities are discouraging visitors.

Tourist offices: London: c/o Colombian Consulate General, Suite 10, 140 Park Lane, London W1Y 3DF; Telephone: 071 493 4565.
Madrid: Calle Princesa No 17, Tercera Izquierda; Telephone: 2485090.

New York: 140 East 57th Street, Telephone: 6880151.

Visa: British passport holders – no visa is required, but a valid passport and a return or onward journey ticket must be produced. Leave to enter for 90 days is usually granted on arrival. USA passport holders – a visa is required and should be applied for at the consulate at least 48 hours in advance, together with return or onward ticket, passport and a recent photograph.

Tourist security: Contact the Foreign Office shortly before departure for the latest situation, although the Colombian government have issued no warnings. Medellín and Cali are very dangerous for foreigners, and caution should be exercised everywhere.

Embassies/Consulates to be contacted in case of tourist difficulty:
British: Torre Propaganda Sancho, Calle 98 No 9-03, Piso 40, Bogotá, D.E.
USA: Calle 38 No. 8-61, Bogotá, D.E.

Languages: The local language is Spanish, but English is spoken in tourist areas.

Currency: Approximate exchange rate, Colombian pesos, £1 = Col$ 1000.00. US dollars preferred. Credit cards and traveller's cheques

38. Main street, Quito, Ecuador. Disability and begging form an uneasy partnership to a background of credit-card-toting jewellery shops.

accepted. Bank opening times: 9 a.m. to 3.30 p.m. Monday to Friday. Black market for US dollars. Gratuities: 10 per cent when not included in the bill. On leaving Colombia, travellers may exchange up to $100 in Colombian pesos, on presentation of passport and currency exchange receipts. Outside Colombia exchange is not recommended.

Electricity: 110/120 volts.

Accommodation: Camping is not considered safe.

Air travel: Most convenient international airport for US and European connections: Eldorado Airport, Bogotá, also Barranquilla and Cali. Internal flights; Avianca has special offers for foreigners travelling to Colombia. Departure tax US$15, payable in dollars.

Car travel: Rental, International Driving Permit, with major credit cards. No speed limits on roads. Car touring club: Automóvil Club de Colombia (ACC) offices at any important city. Road conditions are very poor in most areas. Petrol is widely available. Driving is on the right.

Rail travel on Andean routes: none.

Maps: Best available, in Madrid, New York and locally. 1:100,000, Instituto Geografico, Bogotá.

Medical: No special precautions are necessary unless you are arriving from an infected area or visiting the Amazonas, the Pacific Coast and the Llanes Orientales region, in which case smallpox, yellow fever and malaria prophylactics are required.

Weather: There is no best time of year to visit – Colombia has all climates, all year round. The temperature depends on altitude. Above 3500 m (10,000 ft) it is mostly cold and snow can fall at any time.

Mountaineering club: Club Los Yetis, Ibagué; Campo Abierto, Apartado Aereo 53.670, Diagonal 29, No 37-41 Bogotá.

THE ECUADOREAN ANDES AT A GLANCE

General situation

Ecuador has long been considered one of the most peaceful and quiet Andean nations, and it is reasonably safe, certainly compared to Peru or Colombia. Though Ecuador is politically fairly dormant, street crime is on the increase. Avoid carrying large quantities of cash and other valuables. We still spend two or three times a local farmer's annual salary on a two-week holiday. In Quito care should be taken in the old town and around the Panecillo, and on the steps approaching it, where muggings are frequent. The coastal city of Guayaquil is a major centre for street crime. Women should avoid travelling alone – mixed groups are more likely to avoid sexual harassment.

Capital: Quito

Population: 10 million.

Main Andean ranges: East and West Cordilleras (Oriental and Occidental).

Highest and best known summits: Chimborazo, 6310 m (20,703 ft); Cotopaxi, 5897 m (19,348 ft); Cayambe, 5790 m (18,997 ft); Antisana 5704 m (18,715 ft); El Altar, 5319 m (17,452 ft).

Best known Andean towns/resorts: Quito; Baños; Riobamba; Ambato; Otavalo.

Other features: Avenue of the Volcanoes.

Tourist offices: London: c/o the Embassy of Ecuador, Flat 3b, 3 Hans Crescent, London SW1X 0LS; Telephone: 071 584 1367.
New York: 18 East 41 Street, Room 1800, New York NY 10017; Telephone: (212) 683-7555.

Visa: British passport holders – no visa required up to six-month stay. It is possible the immigration authorities might ask to see a return ticket.

USA passport holders – sight of return ticket may be requested, but no visa is required for stays of up to three months.

Embassies/Consulates to be contacted in case of tourist difficulty:
British: Av. González Suárez 111, Quito; Telephone: 560-309/669/670/671.
USA: Av. Patria 12 de Octubre, Quito; Telephone: 562-890.

Languages: The local language is Spanish. English is spoken in some larger resorts, and is the second language of Ecuador, but do not expect widespread use on the street. Most Indians speak Quechua.

Currency: Approximate exchange rate, £1 = s/.1400 (sucres). Some market for pounds sterling, but dollars preferred. Major credit cards and traveller's cheques accepted. Bank opening times 9 a.m. to 1.30 pm; 2 p.m. to 6 p.m. (cash tills) Monday to Friday. Black market – illegal, but widespread. Local currency cannot be exported and exchanged on return home.

Electricity: 110 volts.

Accommodation: Main tourist centres, e.g. Quito, have all standards from $2 to $50 per night. Elsewhere, good accommodation can be secured at very reasonable prices by European standards, while basic accommodation can be had for $1–2.

Air travel: Most convenient international aiport for US and European connections: Quito. Airport departure tax US$20. Internal flights: about ten daily to Guayaquil (US$12) and Cuenca (US$18). For US$30, the Icaro flying school will organize flights along the Avenue of the Volcanoes.

Car travel: Rental – main international companies operate. Speed limit 60 kph (40 mph). Car touring club Automóvil Club de Ecuador, 218 Eloy Alfaro y Berlin, Quito; Telephone: 02-237779. Road conditions are reasonable on the main routes, but watch out for potholes, even on good roads. Petrol is widely available. Driving is on the right.

Maps: Best available locally, especially the four-page map of Ecuador, available from the Institutio Géografico Militar, one of the best South American maps.

Medical: No inoculations are compulsory.

Weather: Any time is good for a visit, but the weather is best between March and September.

Mountaineering club: Associacion de Excursionismo y Andinismo de Pinchincha, Concentracion Deportiva, Apdo Aereo A, 108, Quito. This club, and others are mainly for Ecuadorean nationals. The South American Explorers Club has a newly opened branch at Apartado 21-43, Eloy Alfaro, Quito. Also available at Box 18327, Denver, Co. 80218 USA; Telephone: (303) 320-0388.

THE PERUVIAN ANDES AT A GLANCE

General situation

The Foreign Office has advised British travellers that terrorism and crime are an everyday reality in Peru. Eighteen thousand lives have been lost in the last decade because of terrorist activities, mainly Sendero Luminoso and MRTA (Túpac Amaru). Both groups attack the government and security forces while MRTA have a reputation for kidnapping and extortion. Usually it is Peruvians who suffer, but in 1988 three foreign aid workers were killed, and in 1989 a British traveller was murdered by terrorists near Huaras. Four tourists have disappeared, presumably killed, on the Nazca/Cuzco road, which passes through the Emergency Zone department of Ayacucho and Apurimac. Travellers are advised to avoid this road at all costs.

39. *Cuzco, Peru. Tourist guide demonstrates the perfection of Inca stonework.*

The Foreign Office should be consulted before travelling. In July 1990 the following departments were in a state of emergency; Apurimac, Ayacucho, Callao Province, Huancavelica, Huánaco, Junín, Lima, Loreto, Pasco, San Martin, Ucayali. The advice is to avoid these areas, even in transit by road or rail. Terrorist activity in Ancash has put the Cordillera Blanca and Huayhuash effectively out of bounds until the situation improves. Cuzco and Macchu Picchu are not in a state of emergency. Thieves and pickpockets are generally active, while the Inca Trail has been the scene of a number of robberies, on one occasion involving loss of life. Tourists walking the Inca Trail are advised not to do so in groups of less than six.

Capital: Lima.

Population: 22 million.

Main Andean ranges: Cordilleras Blanca, Huayuash, Vilcabamba, Urubamba, Vilcanota.

Highest and best known summits: Huascaran Sur 6768 m (22,204 ft); Yerupaja (El Carnicero, the Butcher 6634 m – 21,765 ft); Ausangate 6384 m (20,945 ft); Salcantay 6271 m (20,574 ft).

Best known Andean towns/resorts: Huaras, Cuzco.

Other physical features: The Colca Canyon – deeper than the Grand Canyon; the *Puya raimondii* Altiplano flower, which flowers once every century; Lake Titicaca, shared with Bolivia – the world's highest navigable lake.

Tourist offices: London: 10 Grosvenor Gardens, London SW1W 0BD; Telephone: 071 824 8693. Washington DC: 1700 Massachusetts Avenue NW, Washington, DC 200036; Telephone: 202-833-9860.

Visa: British passport holders – valid passport and return/onward ticket for issue of 60-day visa at the border. USA passport holders – as British.

Embassies/Consulates to be contacted in case of tourist difficulty: British: Natalio Sanchez 125, 11th Floor, Lima; Telephone: 33 47 38. Emergency bleeper service – Telephone: 32 09 82.
USA: Grimaldo del Solar 346, Miraflores; Telephone: 443621.

Language: The local language is Spanish, but many Indians speak Quechua. English is occasionally spoken in some larger tourist centres, e.g. Lima and Cuzco.

Currency: The Peruvian sol has been replaced by the Inti, worth 1000 soles. Approximate exchange rate, US$1 = 20 Intis. Dollars are preferred. Gratuities vary between 10 and 30 per cent. Credit cards and traveller's cheques are accepted in major tourist centres. Bank opening times: 8.30 a.m. to 11.30 a.m. weekday mornings only. Black market flourishes. Local currency can be exchanged on departure if currency exchange receipts are presented, but it is useless on return home.

40. Simple accommodation, Pisaq, near Cuzco, Peru.

Electricity: 220 volts.

Accommodation: covers the whole spectrum, from US$2 hovels in poor country areas to US$50 luxury hotels in Lima and Cuzco, which also have their share of middle-range accommodation.

Air travel: The most convenient international airport for US and European connections is Lima, where there is a fair internal network of domestic flights, especially useful to Nazca and Cuzco and areas where ground travel is not currently recommended. Aeroperu and Faucett are the main carriers, but beware of overbooking in peak season. Double check everything and arrive early to claim your seat. Airport departure tax is US$15, payable in dollars.

Car travel in Peru is an adventure into heat, cold, mud and dust. Only the Pan American Highway (running north–south by the coast) and a few stretches of inland road are paved and resemble the roads to which we are accustomed. The rest are dirt tracks. Landslides, road blocks, even highway robbery are not unknown. Plenty of adventure can be had on local buses, and for local journeys taxis are cheap by our standards. Car rental is more expensive than in the UK, and is operated by the main international companies. Four-wheel drive is necessary for most roads. There are few traffic signals, signposts and speed limits, and these are usually ignored. Car touring club: Peruvian Touring Club, 699 Cesar Vallejo, Lima; Telephone: 40-3270. 95 octane petrol is cleaner than the 84 octane. Driving is on the right.

Rail travel on Andean routes includes the Cuzco–Macchu Picchu line, the Cuzco–Juliaca–Puno route along the Altiplano, the central and southern Peruvian Andean lines, which reach 4700 m (15,600 ft).

Maps: Institutio Geografico Militar 1/100,000.

Weather: The best time of year to visit is from May to September, especially for trekking in the mountains. This is the driest time, the Andean winter. The rest of the year can be unpredictable and very wet, hindering road and rail travel and any mountaineering expedition.

Mountaineering club: Club Andino, Las Begonias 630, San Isidro, Lima 27. South American Explorers Club, Av Portugal 146 (Brena), Lima 100; Telephone: 31-4480. Also available at Box 18327, Denver, Co. 80218 USA; Telephone: (303) 320-0388.

THE BOLIVIAN ANDES AT A GLANCE

> ## General situation
>
> Bolivia is one of the safer Andean countries for foreign visitors, with no significant terrorist problem. There is, however, a massive drug trade, which travellers would be well advised to steer clear of; foreigners can languish for years without trial in Bolivian jails. Care should also be taken when approached by so-called 'plainclothes policemen'. Check identity in all cases. The general South American caution against pickpockets in crowded places applies in Bolivia. The country is politically unstable, but the frequent changes of government affect very few people outside the main square of La Paz.

Population: 7 million

Capital: La Paz

Main Andean ranges: Cordilleras Real, Oriental.

Highest and best known summits: Illimani 6462 m (21,201 ft); Illampu 6380 m (20,931 ft); Huayna Potosi 6090 m (19,980 ft).

Best known Andean towns/resorts: La Paz; Potosí.

Other physical features: Lake Titicaca, the world's highest navigable lake.

Tourist offices: London: c/o Bolivian Embassy, 106 Eaton Square, London W1; Telephone: 071 235 4248.
Washington: c/o Bolivian Embassy, 3014 Massachusetts Avenue NW Washington, DC 20008; Telephone: 202-483 4410.

Visa: British passport holders – none required for a stay of up to 30 days.
USA passport holders – none required for a stay of up to 90 days.

Tourist security: generally good.

Embassies/Consulates to be contacted in case of tourist difficulty:
British: Avenida Arce 2732, La Paz; Telephone: 329401.
USA: Calle Colon, Mercado, La Paz; Telephone: 02-350120

Languages: The local language is Spanish, with some Quechua, although most Indians speak Aymara. English is not widely spoken, a little in tourist hotels in La Paz.

Currency: The Boliviano (Bs). Approximate exchange rate, - Bs 2.50 = US$1. Dollars are preferred; pounds sterling are almost unheard of. Gratuities: 10 per cent, none for taxis. Few credit cards are accepted but there are some American Express and Visa outlets in the capital. Bank opening times: 9.00 a.m.–12 p.m.; 2.00 p.m.–4.00 p.m., they are very slow for currency exchange. Black markets – flourishing, but with the normal risks. The Boliviano is worthless outside the country.

Electricity: 220 volts.

Accommodation: All standards are available in La Paz, from international luxury to basic beds.

Air travel: The most convenient international airport for US and European connections is El Alto Airport, La Paz. Airport departure tax: US$10. Internal flights with Lloyd Aereo Boliviano are available daily to most major cities.

Car travel: Only really feasible with a four-wheel drive vehicle outside the rainy season, roughly November to March. Car hire is available from local firms on presentation of an International Driving Permit. Petrol is not widely available, and there are long queues for fuel. Driving is on the right.

Rail travel on Andean routes: two lines join the Chilean coast to the Altiplano; Arica–La Paz and Antofagasta–Uyuni and beyond to Potosí, connecting with La Paz.

Maps: Best available are from the Institutio Geografico Militar, Av. 16 de Julio 1471.

Weather: November to February is the wettest period, best avoided. The best (driest) time of year to visit is from May to September.

Mountaineering club: Club Andino Boliviano, Calle Mexico 1638, PO Box 1346, La Paz.

THE CHILEAN ANDES AT A GLANCE

General situation

Chile is generally a safe country for English and American tourists, but they are advised to take sensible precautions regarding valuables and passport – i.e. carry them in a money-belt and use hotel safe deposit where appropriate. After 16 years of the Pinochet dictatorship, democracy has finally returned to Chile, with a freer atmosphere for Chileans and travellers alike.

Capital: Santiago de Chile.

Population: 13 million.

Main Andean ranges: shared with Argentina along the long mountain border – Cordillera Occidental; Paine Horns.

Highest and best known summit: Ojos de Salado 6870 m (22,539 ft), the highest volcano in the world; Cerro Paine 3050 m (10,006 ft), one of the highest rock walls, 1200 m (3936 ft) in the world.

Best known Andean towns/resorts: Portillo, Valle Nevado, Farrelones, Termas de Chillan.

Other features: Longest and narrowest country in the world, and the longest seacoast (6000 km – 4000 miles); Perito Moreno glacier is one of the few glaciers in the world that is still growing.

Tourist offices: London: 12 Devonshire Street, London W1N 2DS; Telephone: 071 580 1023. New York: 866 United Nations Plaza, Suite 302, NY 10017.

Visa: not required by British or USA passport holders.

Embassies/Consulates to be contacted in case of tourist difficulty:
British: La Concepción, 4th Floor, Santiago de Chile; Telephone: 2239166.
USA: Merced 230, Santiago; Telephone: 710133.

Languages: The local language is Spanish, but English is spoken in some larger resorts.

Currency: Approximate exchange rate: 110 Chilean Pesos = £1.00. US dollars obtain the best exchange rate. Gratuities: restaurants add 10 per cent to the bill, but waiters expect a further 10 per cent in addition to this. Major credit cards and traveller's cheques accepted. Bank opening times: 9.00 a.m.–2.00 p.m. Monday to Friday.

Electricity: 220 volts AC

Accommodation: Most types of accommodation are available from $10 per night to top luxury hotels at prices in excess of $100. You may camp in the national parks for a fee. A list of tourist campsites in the country is available from the Santiago tourist office.

Air travel: Most convenient international airport for US and European connections: Padahuel (Santiago). Airport departure tax: US$12.50 international; US$5.00 on domestic. Internal flights with LAN Chile.

Car travel: Rental: International Driving Permit required. Car touring club: Automovil Club de Chile, 195 Pedro de Valdivia, Santiago; Telephone: 02 225 7253. Driving is on the right.

Maps: Best available from the IGM, Nueva Santa Isabel, 1640 Santiago.

Medical: No mandatory health requirements for entry.

Weather: The best time of year to visit is September to April in the central region of Chile. May to August is the rainy season. The lake district has an alpine climate, with snow blocking high passes in the winter (our summer). In the far south, Chilean Patagonia can be cold and windy at any time of year.

Mountaineering club: Federacion de Andinismo de Chile, Vicuna Mackenna 44, Casilla 2239, Santiago.

THE ARGENTINE ANDES AT A GLANCE

General situation

Relations between England and Argentina have improved considerably since the Falklands (Malvinas) war, with many Argentines accepting the conflict as an unfortunate mistake. English tourists are now generally received with politeness and made welcome. Argentina is a generally safe place for foreign travellers, although the incidence of pickpocketing, mugging, baggage theft at airports and even highway robbery (including cars) is on the increase. However, tourists employing common sense can expect a safe trip. The Argentine Embassy in London reopened in May 1990, followed by a tourism attaché in September 1990, giving every sign that Argentina wishes to put herself back on the map, politically and for tourism. This is fortunate indeed since the country has a lot to offer, not least in the Andes.

Capital: Buenos Aires.

Population: 32 million.

Main Andean ranges: The Andes run along the Chile-Argentine border; Fitzroy Massif, Cordilleras de Lipez, Aconcagua, Ramada, Penitentes; Hielo Patagonia Norte and Sur.

Highest and best known summits: Aconcagua 6980 m (22,900 ft) – highest summit in South America and the western hemisphere; Tupungato 6500 m (21,325 ft); Almacenes 5600 m (18,400 ft); Catedral 5300 m (17,388 ft).

Best known Andean towns/resorts: Mendoza, Las Leñas, San Martin De Los Andes, San Carlos de Bariloche.

Main lakes: Lago Nahuel Huapi, Lago San Martin.

Tourist offices: London: c/o Argentine Embassy, 53 Hans Place, London SW1X 0LA; Telephone: 071 584 6494.
New York: 330 West 56th Street, NY 10019; Telephone: (212) 765 8834.

Visa: British passport holders – no visa required; USA passport holders – visa to be obtained at any Argentine consulate.

Embassies/Consulates to be contacted in case of tourist difficulty:
British: Contact the Foreign Office in London prior to departure.
USA: Av. Colombia 4300, Capital Federal (Cp1425); Telephone: 774-7611/9911.

Languages: The local language is Spanish. Do not expect English to be spoken even in larger resorts.

Currency: Approximate exchange rate, the Austral (A); 5200 (A) = $1; 9400 = £1 (was £1 = 1,029 a year ago). US dollars, cash preferred to traveller's cheques, which are not particularly welcome. Credit cards and traveller's cheques accepted, but their use can be suspended in times of economic crisis (quite frequent – inflation is endemic). Bank opening times: 10.00 a.m.–3.00 p.m. Monday to Friday.

Electricity: 220 volts

Accommodation: A good selection of inexpensive and top quality accommodation, availability depending on the season. Camping is possible in the most important resorts.

Air travel: Most convenient international airport for US and European connections: Ezeiza, Buenos Aires; domestic and South American flights – Aeroparque Metropolitano Jorge Newbery. Internal flights – Austral; Aerolineas Argentinas; Pluna; LAPA. Two internal airpasses for tourists, have to be purchased in the country of origin; Visit Argentina I – US$290, six flights in 30 days. Visit Argentina II – US$199, three flights in 15 days.

Car travel: Rental – Hertz, Avis, most major companies at Buenos Aires. Speed limits on roads vary with the region. Car touring club: Automovil Club Argentino (ACA), 1850 Av. del Libertador, Buenos Aires; Telephone: 01-802-0522. Road conditions are generally fair. Petrol is widely available. Driving is on the right.

Maps: Best available locally, at Automovil Club Argentino, or the IGM, Buenos Aires, 1:100,000.

Medical: No mandatory health requirements for entry. Public health standards are generally high, tap water is drinkable in most major cities, and there are few endemic diseases. In the tropical north, precautions should be taken against malaria and chagas.

Weather: The best time of year to visit for skiing is July and August. Generally, the best time is in the Argentine spring and summer, i.e. September to March.

Mountaineering club: Federacion Argentina de Montanismo y Afines, José P Varela 3948, Buenos Aires.

CHAPTER 7 Photography

That well-known Alpine success story, Edward Whymper, was one of the first to bring home images of the Andes after landing in Ecuador in 1879/80. He was not a photographer, but an explorer, mountaineer and artist of considerable merit. Trained as a wood engraver, his engravings of the Ecuadorean Andes and her people are unrivalled by photography even today.

It is a fortunate person who expects to make more than one trip to the Andes. Not surprisingly a large part of the budget is allocated to photography in order to relive the memory, and even perhaps sell photographs to recoup some of the trip's expenses. Photographic opportunities rarely repeat themselves, so one should work on the basis that each trip is the only trip. Each photograph must count, but there is many a slip 'twixt the shot and the print'.

Unfortunately, all the modern technology in the world – autofocus, motordrives, fast film, coated lenses, trick filters and talking cameras – still cannot guarantee any more than a mediocre photograph, whether it be at sea level, on the beach, or on the ski slopes and glaciers of the Andes. Good images from the mountains will always require infinite patience, a good sense of composition, and quite often a good pair of legs to get you to the places other tourists do not reach.

Photographic magazines frequently extol the virtues of the very latest camera that will supposedly make holiday photography easy. Ask a professional and he or she will tell you that all you need is one camera that you use regularly and are comfortable with. Once you have found it, stick to it and concentrate on your technique. It is the photographer, not the camera, who makes the picture.

Photography in the Andes is not just about high mountain photography. It is also about capturing images of local people in the markets, avoiding camera thieves and getting your film home safely. In short, these are the tricks of travel photography on the road, tinged with an element of danger and adventure. Many pitfalls await the Andean photographer. Inevitably the most interesting locations – markets, Inca ruins, sunrises and sunsets – attract the criminal element and are favourite haunts of camera thieves and bag snatchers. See the section on personal security in the chapter 'Visiting the Andes'.

Immediately a conflict arises for the photographer planning a trip to the Andes. It is a long way from home, the likelihood of a second trip is remote, and the chances of theft are high. Also local film and equipment are often expensive and of poor quality. Think very hard about

41. *The town of Pisaq, Sacred Valley of the Incas, near Cuzco, Peru.*

whether you wish to bother with photography at all – leaving your camera at home may save a number of headaches.

If an Andean trip without a camera is inconceivable, however, either take a camera whose loss will not matter much, or take the best available, check insurance and know the procedures for reporting a possible theft and making a claim. Remember that a camera costing between £200 and £500 may represent a year's salary in some Andean countries. Waving it around in a market may be more provocation than thieves can resist – and can you blame them? So be warned. A healthy awareness of these facts will increase the chances of your film and camera returning home in one piece.

Some basic precautions will help. I do not recommend the use of camera bags on an Andean trip – it is too clear from a distance what the contents are. A functional but grubby

42. Campesina, *Ecuador.*

bag is ideal, or disguise a camera bag inside a plastic or woven bag of local manufacture. Whatever bag you use, reinforce the shoulder strap so that it cannot be cut with a knife and snatched. A second safety strap around your waist or attached to your belt is an additional security.

Although it is less comfortable, learn to carry a camera bag/daypack in front where you can see it at all times. This avoids having your bag slashed behind your back with razor blades – it happens so quickly that it is often unnoticed until later. At the Cuzco station for Macchu Picchu I entered the station with five other travellers. We ran a gauntlet of jostling and pushing that lasted perhaps 20 seconds before we were safely on the platform. In this time

three bags were slashed, two cameras stolen. None of the victims had noticed a thing.

Exposed film should be left in a safe place – ideally in a hotel safe – only carry enough for each day's photography. When relaxing at restaurants, cafés, etc., place bags out of sight, away from streets and windows, with the strap looped under a table or chair leg. These precautions apply at all times, especially in crowded places such as bus and railway stations. Avoid changing lenses and films out in the open – the risk is greatest while you are distracted. Accept that it is a bore to have to take these precautions, but do it from the start so that theft avoidance becomes a habit, even a way of life. Then there is some chance you will be able to relax enough to take good photographs.

Markets and fiestas occur almost daily in the Andes, when colourful local people come in from the countryside to trade, barter and pass

43. Pisaq, near Cuzco, Peru.

the time. They offer fantastic photographic opportunities – stalls bursting with fresh fruit, livestock from pig to guinea pig for the pot, weavings and textiles, bowler-hatted ladies with babies swaddled in blazing ponchos; weathered faces that speak volumes of the hard struggle for existence in a mountain valley or the windswept Altiplano. The pain and the glory of the Andes is in front of your lens, waiting to be captured and brought home.

Capturing it is less easy. One does not encounter the Asian belief in the camera stealing the soul, but the Andean reaction is mixed. Some are just plain offended – after all how would we feel in the supermarket being surrounded by hordes of snap-happy foreigners? Many look away and present an uninspiring back view. Some become angry.

95

44. Professional poser above Cuzco, Peru.

Others ask for money, particularly those in traditional dress leading a well-groomed llama. This combination is seen at many a tourist location, and is truly and unashamedly 'professional'. They have dressed themselves and their llamas in order to be photographed. They expect to be paid and will pursue you mercilessly until you do pay. The morality of this leaves something to be desired, and examining it opens up far wider issues of why we travel, and the effect we have on economically poorer locals when we do. Be that as it may, if you are seen photographing a professional llama poser, expect to pay for the privilege.

I have found the best way to obtain good candid market/people photographs is to shoot from the waist with a pre-set wide angle lens and hope for the best. This is more suited to black and white photography where the composition and framing can be remedied in the darkroom back home. Alternatively, use a right-angle viewfinder, which makes it less obvious to the subject that they are being photographed. A third possibility is to use a long lens and find a secluded spot such as a window, roof or staircase above a market – almost a hide – and pick off your subjects at your leisure and without them becoming agitated. Avoid photographing airports and military institutions – most Andean countries are very touchy about this.

In the Andes the contrast between bright sunlight and shade is often extreme, whether on the Altiplano, in towns or in the mountains. Unless you are happy for shaded areas to come out black in your photographs, try and avoid scenes that contain too much shade, either in landscapes or in markets, where faces are often hidden under hats or stall covers and all detail is lost in the print. The problem is particularly bad with colour transparency film in the middle of the day when the sun is high and the contrast at its greatest. The best times for general photography are early in the morning and late in the evening, or on bright overcast days when the light levels are still quite high but contrast is less.

A solution in the markets would be to use fill-in flash. The flash should be set so that the shadows are within two stops of the bright sunlight exposure. Thus if the sunlight exposure is f16, set an automatic flash to f8. The result will be a less contrasty scene, with detail in the shadows without looking artificial. The problem, of course, is that the flash immediately advertises your presence, but it does promise a better result. Those who are unwilling to carry the extra equipment had better stick to scenes with less contrast, or get in close with a long lens and expose only for the main subject matter.

As with any article of value taken on an Andean trip, it is wise to carry with you a photocopy of the original purchase receipt. You will need this in the event of an insurance claim and it can help with any customs queries on returning home.

BASIC EQUIPMENT

A 35 mm single lens reflex camera is the best compromise of weight, adaptability and quality. If you decide to pursue photography as a hobby, interchangeable lenses and attachments can be built onto the basic body bit by bit. Simple mechanical cameras with mechanical shutters are better in the mountains than cameras in which everything works by batteries. These always let you down when you most need them.

Lenses

The best all-purpose lenses are the 28 mm and 35 mm lenses, which give a fairly wide-angled view and reasonable depth of field, within which everything is in focus. The 50 mm lens is often described as the lens that most nearly corresponds to the natural perspective seen by the human eye, but I find it neither telephoto nor wide angle enough to be much use as a standard lens.

The 105 mm and 135 mm lenses are very useful as medium telephoto lenses while not being too heavy nor having too little depth of field. Lenses of 200 mm, 300 mm and over are excellent for creating tightly cropped views of distant scenes, animals, walkers on a ridge, but are often too heavy to be carried conveniently on the camera. Thus they are rarely to hand when needed quickly and mostly require a slow shutter speed and tripod to obtain an image without camera shake.

Zoom lenses used to be inferior to prime (fixed focal length) lenses, but for most cases a good zoom is now indistinguishable from a prime lens. You can save weight by carrying a zoom, although zooms can lead to a great deal of wasted film because of framing indecision.

Basic filters

Whatever lenses you use, a skylight filter should be left on the camera at all times. This cuts out haze and a little of the blue light so prevalent at high altitude, as well as protecting the lens. Other basic filters I carry are a polarizing filter and a 25A deep red filter. The polarizer is most effective at 90 degrees to the sun, when it will darken the blue sky, penetrate haze, enhance bright colours and suppress reflections. Open your lens aperture by one and a half stops to allow for the filter, e.g. from f11/f16 to f8. The deep red filter needs a three-stop increase in

exposure (e.g. f16 to f5.6). It also darkens blue sky to black, whitens clouds, and penetrates haze, producing dramatic effects in black and white photography.

Best compromise

I have found the best compromise for the committed mountain and travel photographer is to have two identical or similar camera bodies, one loaded with colour, one with black and white film. Lenses can be interchanged. If one is damaged, the other is always available as a spare. Smaller automatic cameras are fine for snaps, but lenses cannot be changed, filters are not always available. Also, the extent of manual control, so essential for a good result rather than a machine-induced fluke, is limited.

Keep it simple. My basic equipment is two Nikon camera bodies, a 35 mm and 105 mm lens with skylight filters, a polarizer and 25A red filter. One reason for cutting down on lenses is that you need only carry one size of filter. Cameras can easily be carried around your neck or in specially designed 'camera care' type pouches on the waist band of a backpack.

Exposure

Automatic cameras and cameras with exposure meters are very useful if the sun is coming from behind you and the subject matter is of average reflectivity, which manufacturers call 18 per cent grey. Most subjects are not that obliging.

45. *Shanty housing and colonial splendour beneath the natural magnificence of El Altar, Riobamba, Ecuador. A 105 mm lens brings together varying aspects of the landscape, despite their different distances from the camera.*

If you are pointing your camera at the sun, at a snowslope or at a dark forest of pines, your automatic exposure meter will give an inaccurate result.

Two things have to be considered. First, how much light is falling on the subject from behind the camera – the incident light? Second, how much light is being reflected from the subject – the reflected light? As a general rule, the right setting will be achieved if you can find an average subject lit with the same light as your subject. Take a reading from this and use it as a guide for the main picture. This is explained in more detail below when I discuss photography on the snow.

Try to select subjects without too much difference between light and dark areas, since the exposure range of most films will not be able to record all the details in highlight or shade. As a general rule, when using negative (print film), err if anything on the side of overexposure (give the film plenty of light) so that there is detail in the shadows. With colour transparency film (slides) concentrate on the highlights, the brightest areas. Err on the side of underexposure. Do not allow the highlights to 'burn out' because of too much light reaching the film.

Other formats

Professional landscape photographers still carry large format cameras into the mountains, as did their forebears, since this is still the best way to obtain top quality for maximum enlargement. Medium format cameras such as the Hasselblad offer a good compromise of quality and portability. But where action photography is required, the 35 mm SLR camera is still the best. While producing remarkable results for their size and portability, 110 and disc cameras are great for snaps but not much else. Frankly, in the Andes any format larger than 35 mm is likely to be unworkable, from the point of view of time, bulk, weight and security. Mobility is the key. Your equipment needs to be with you

the whole time. The ability to carry large format equipment in the Andes would be enviable, but not feasible without an assistant or crew on a trip whose only or main purpose is photography.

46. *El Altar from Parque 21 Abril, Riobamba, Ecuador. Close cropping with a 105 mm lens adds punch and drama to this evening landscape under a threatening sky.*

Tripod for landscapes

One of the simplest ways to improve the quality of your landscapes is to use a tripod for any static subject. Not only does this eliminate the possibility of camera shake – more likely than you think at altitude when your heart is pumping with the exertion of a climb – but also it will enable you to use a slow shutter speed, thus achieving maximum depth of field and keeping everything in focus. Again, the Andean problem is portability. You might get away

with a light tripod with a stone-bag tied between the legs – the additional weight will make it steadier.

A variety of filters can be used in an attempt to improve the conditions as you find them. But none can really improve on what God can do on a good day. One of the basic tenets of landscape photography is to represent the landscape as it is rather than as a manipulated image of composite filters and tricks. Filters have their place – a graduated filter is useful for darkening

a part of the sky too bright to register on film – but as a general rule they are an irrelevancy to landscape photography.

IN SEARCH OF THE ENDURING LANDSCAPE

I cannot tell you what to photograph but some general guidelines may help you to obtain some better than average images.

Aerials

Your first chance of good Andean views may occur even before you arrive on your inward flight. Having worked out the geography of your approach, secure a window seat. Set your shutter speed to at least 1/500th of a second,

47. *An otherwise fine view of Nevado Veronica is scarred by telegraph wires. Taken from the Macchu Picchu train, near Cuzco, Peru. For the best angles you have to get out and walk.*

cut out reflections with a sweater or jacket against the window and over your head. Set the focus at infinity, but avoid letting the camera touch the window. You may have some surprising results. Internal flights are a good source too. Ask when checking in if your flight path passes volcanoes or snow peaks and secure a suitable window seat.

The magic hours

The 'magic hours' of dawn and dusk often produce the most interesting light in the moun-

tains, but this requires either a very early start or missing out on dinner. You have to be a committed photographer to catch this light, but it is usually worth it, particularly in winter when the only colour is white snow. In the middle of the day, overhead light gives little drama to the mountains, whereas a low morning or evening light etches character into any scene.

Heavy weather drama

Bad weather produces the most dramatic scenes and lighting, so whatever the weather, keep your camera handy, wrapped if necessary in a plastic bag. A slow shutter speed, say 1/30th of a second, will blur falling snow or rain for an epic photograph. Learn to work quickly, since the clouds change everything in seconds and mountains really do go away, not to reappear for days. You rarely get a second chance in the mountains.

48. Pisaq, near Cuzco, Peru. The 105 mm lens is ideal for showing middle distance landscapes.

Work for the angle

When on climbing, walking and skiing trips, try and get ahead or to the side of the action for the best angles. Too many shots of these sports just show backs of heads and bottoms. Use a fast shutter speed, say 1/500th of a second, for action. It is best to pre-focus on a spot and wait for the action to come to you.

In search of inspiration

Study magazines and brochures of your favourite mountain sports. Try and work out what it is you like about the photographs that most impress you. With practice you can work out lenses, filters, shutter speeds and aperture stop just by looking at the photograph. When you are

in the mountains, think in terms of photographic opportunities. You will learn to feel them developing. You can take photographs in your head, practising even without a camera.

For pure landscape, never pass up a chance to see exhibitions of mountain paintings, modern and ancient. Admittedly the painter can always place a village or a peak where they will, but the proportions, the perspectives and the sense of drama will add to your visual vocabulary and spark off new ideas and opportunities.

Think before you shoot

The real difference between professional and amateur is that, on the whole, professionals have to satisfy the demands of their clients. Consciously or unconsciously, they are always asking the question 'Why am I taking this shot?' The result is that the picture works. Professionals know and care for their equipment

49. Campesinas *and camera-shy child. Latacunga, Ecuador. A 200 mm lens holds the subjects away from the background.*

like old friends. Like old friends, their equipment can be relied on. Good photography is really about being in control of the result; that's how they stay in business. But non-professionals, understandably, have less time to practise.

Before leaving home

First check your camera. Clean it, put in new batteries, run a short roll of film through and check the results. Decide what equipment you want to take to the slopes. Most importantly, keep gear to a minimum. Otherwise it will be left in the hotel. Get organized and you are half-way down the slope towards good photography.

It may be far better to carry just one compact camera, rather than a backpack full of gear that you will not have the time to use. Admittedly, when on a professional assignment, I would carry at least two camera bodies, one for colour and one for black and white, a selection of lenses, and maybe a spare body too. But then I'm not on holiday, you are! So do not over burden yourself.

Film

Decide how much film you will probably use, then take twice as much. You can always bring it home again. Locally they are almost always out of the film you want, and what is left is expensive or out of date. This is a particular risk in Andean countries – it is not unknown to be sold a stolen exposed film! I always take my camera gear as hand luggage; it is then safe from theft or breakage *en route*, though not safe, perhaps, from airport X-rays.

Personally, I do not trust X-ray machines. I always ask for a hand search and have all my film ready to be opened and examined, I generally go through the departure gate 30 minutes early just for this reason! Kodak say that only repeated exposure to X-rays will cause a problem. If you prefer a quiet life, take the risk. But if you want to be in total control of your results from start to finish, then the answer must be obvious. With the increase in terrorism, the chances of being allowed to have your baggage hand-searched are small. If prior enquiry suggests film will have to be X-rayed, the best solution would seem to be to place your film with your checked baggage. Whereas European X-ray systems are becoming safer for film, many Andean countries use old-fashioned high-power machines that are almost guaranteed to ruin film.

I always use the slowest film possible for the lighting conditions. Snow scenes have a lot of reflected light, which means you can use Kodachrome 25 or 64. If you want to shoot action, and have some depth of field in the background, you will need 200 ASA or even 400 ASA film. Fujichrome film gives bright colours, which clean whites for snow and is one of my favourites in the mountains. If your final aim is to have photographs published in magazines, always use transparencies for colour, and print film for black and white. Kodachrome is a good film for the Andes. It travels well, does not need to be processed immediately and is fast enough for most of the bright light conditions likely to be encountered. Avoid local processing, unless there is an accredited Kodak laboratory. Posting Kodak to a home laboratory may be a solution, but there is the risk of postal loss as well as postal security X-rays, which are even more lethal than at airports.

IN THE MOUNTAINS

Snow photography

The mountain environment can be as hostile as any to the making of good pictures. Temperatures down to $-35°C$, howling winds, frozen hands, dead batteries, snapping film, static electricity, and a background that is about as far away from 18 per cent grey as it could be – these are just some of the problems that the mountain photographer may encounter. Unfortunately it is more likely to be the photographer who is to blame for a disappointing result and not the equipment. So here are some hot tips for cold pictures, to put the white back into your snow, the blue back into the sky and those sparkling eyes back into your snow photography.

On the snow, start with looking after yourself. You will never take good pictures if you are not comfortable and warm, especially your hands. It might help to use a very thin second glove under your ski glove, so you can use the camera and still keep warm. Carry your camera where it is easily accessible and can be kept warm and dry if you fall. If the camera becomes cold, even new batteries may fail. If your camera

50. Chimborazo, Ecuador 6310 m (20,703 ft). Four climbers can just be seen below the skyline of the summit ridge.

is fully automatic, that is the end of photography until you can warm it up again. If you anticipate very cold conditions, get your camera winterized so that the oil does not freeze.

Batteries in motordrives can also suffer. Film becomes brittle when cold and can snap on winding. Also, dry mountain air is highly charged with static electricity. This can cause sparks inside the camera body that will blemish the film. Wind and re-wind slowly by hand.

Snow exposure

Exposure is a common problem on the snow. Being calibrated to an average grey, most metering will tend to underexpose snow pictures. The meter thinks there is more light available than

there actually is. There are a number of ways around this problem.

You could do worse than to rely on the manufacturers' recommendations for snow scenes. Or you can fill the frame of a TTL (through the lens) meter camera with a grey or neutrally coloured anorak, a tanned face, or the back of your hand and then lock on this reading for the general scene. If you carry a meter, take an incident light reading, which will be unaffected by the glare of a predominantly white scene. All of these methods will be more accurate than blindly relying on TTL metering.

Set your camera manually. Those with automatic cameras may have to lock the exposure, or fool the meter by adjusting the exposure compensation dial to +2. Alternatively, you can adjust the ASA rating to one stop slower than the film that is actually loaded, i.e. 100 ASA instead of 200 ASA.

These dodges only apply when the scene is dominated by snow. If you are taking a full frame close up, then go back to the normal TTL metering. For further insurance, bracket your exposures to either side of the indicated reading. Most professionals do this whenever the shot is important. Another safeguard is to use colour negative film rather than transparency. An exposure that is one stop out can still be adequately printed back home, whereas the smaller latitude of transparency film is such that the shot may be lost because of inaccurate exposure.

Many professionals argue that photography begins, not ends, when the shutter is released. By all means shoot more film, but show less. Select the best from your pictures and have them enlarged. Better by far to show ten really good shots than three rolls of mediocrity. If you get some really good ones, why not put them on the wall?

CHAPTER 8 Train

'The iron fingers of a railroad, if attached to the hand of Lima, would instantly squeeze out all the wealth of the Andes, and the whistle of the locomotives would awaken the Indian race from its centuries-old lethargy.'

Thus spoke President Balta of Peru in 1868. His prophesy was fulfilled throughout the whole of the Andes. English and American speculators and railway pioneers opened up the whole mountain chain, transporting the rich mineral deposits to the Pacific coast for shipment to foreign lands.

The Andean railways are some of the finest examples of railway engineering in the world, but do not expect European timings and standards of comfort. For those with a limited budget and time on their hands, who are prepared to take their comfortable holidays back home, seeing the Andes by train is to see them as the local people do. Those who have read Theroux's *Old Patagonian Express* will have enjoyed the humour and the frustrations of an attempt to travel the length of two continents by train, and you will have many stories of your own.

Local trains are slow, cheap and uncomfortable, but fun. The term *expreso* has no connection with speed. Pack your sense of humour, forget all notions of timekeeping (a 400 km – 250 mile journey could take a day and a night), be kind to chickens and pigs, keep your eyes on your bags, and there is every chance of an enjoyable trip. Pullman or buffet cars tend to

be safest from the security point of view. First and second class are often the worst seats on the train, and indistinguishable for quality!

Many of the northern trans-Andean lines were built to transport raw materials from the world's highest mines to the Pacific coast. As a rule the services of the northern Andes are more ramshackle and slower than those in the south – particularly Chile and Argentina, which have classic, albeit dated, rolling stock and even air-conditioning.

One dominant feature of Andean railways is that they tend to drop out of action for a few years and then re-appear on the scene again. I have described the main Andean train trips that are in existence and that, given good luck and an absence of guerrilla activity, earthquake, landslip and breakdown, may provide a memorable traverse of the Andes.

VENEZUELA

In Venezuela trains are given low priority, and the only mountain railway is the cable railway from Caracas to Mount Avila. The Mérida to Pico Espejo cable car has one of the longest spans in the world.

COLOMBIA

The 3600 km (2300 miles) of Colombian tracks have currently been restricted to freight only, pending a major reorganization of the passenger network. The exception is the weekend steam train (*tren turistico*) from Bogota to Nemocón, and its diesel continuation to Chinquinquira through the Colombian highlands. The trip takes about seven hours and travellers can return the next day by diesel train. There is an intermittent passenger service from Santa Marta

51. The Cuzco-Macchu Picchu train, Peru.

to Bogota that climbs from sea level to 2640 m (8661 ft).

ECUADOR

A local train service runs daily from Quito to Riobamba, giving excellent views of the Avenue of the Volcanoes, the name given by Humboldt to the two spectacular ranges of volcanic snow-peaks that flank the fertile valleys of central

Ecuador. West of Riobamba, the coastal section of this 460 km (290 mile) line climbs from sea level to the Urbina pass at 3609 m (11,800 ft). Part of the coastal section of the line to Guayaquil was washed away by extensive landslides – the effects of El Niño and the torrential rains of 1983 – and had not been replaced by late 1989. Some progress, albeit slow, is being made. The most spectacular section is the climb from the coastal delta to 3283 m (10,800 ft) gaining 3000 m (10,000 ft) altitude in only 80 km (50 miles). Despite the altitude gain, the maximum gradient of the 1.067 m (2 ft 11 in) gauge railway is 5.5 per cent, achieved mostly by the Alausi loop and the Devil's Nose zigzags.

When fully open, the Guayaquil to Quito railway is arguably one of the great railway journeys of the world. It starts on the fertile tropical coastal plains with views of waterbirds in the sugar cane fields and rice paddies, travels past coffee, banana, mango and breadfruit plantations to the base of the Andes, through the Chanchan gorge and over the Nariz del Diablo (the Devil's Nose mountain).

After Alausí, steep slopes give way to the desolate *páramo* moor thence to the high plateau with superb views of the snowcapped volcanoes – Chimborazo (Ecuador's highest peak), Cotopaxi (the highest active volcano in the world), El Altar, Tungurahua and smoking Sangay.

The Avenue of the Volcanoes section can be sampled on the Quito–Riobamba return journey, it costs US$2, and takes about five hours each way. Metropolitan Tours organize a two-day round trip with a special luxury carriage, with overnight in Riobamba and side-trips to Indian markets for US$120, returning by bus. But the full trip from Guayaquil on the coast would be better still – even with buses filling in the current gaps in the train track – since this gives the true impression of how the Andes and the South American continent rise from the coast – and how flora, fauna and the people change with the altitude.

In common with much of the rest of South America, the facilities on the train are basic, not particularly comfortable, cold at night and crowded. Seats should be booked well in advance.

PERU

The Peruvian network has shrunk markedly since the 1970 earthquake, particularly in the north, and much is unlikely to be reopened. The lines were built mainly in the nineteenth century by British and American companies, using Chinese labourers. Indeed the British ran many of the lines until the early 1960s. Today Peru has three main railway trips – the Macchu Picchu line; the central Andean line and the southern Andean line. Day trains are an excellent way to see the scenery, while night trains are an excellent way to be relieved of your baggage, so exercise caution at all times, and ideally do not travel alone.

Cuzco–Macchu Picchu

The undoubted lure of the 'Lost City of the Incas' taps into everyone's imagination and makes the Cuzco–Macchu Picchu line the most frequented tourist attraction in the Andes. Two diesel trains ply this route: the 'tourist' train, which is faster, cleaner, safer, later and more expensive – and the 'local' train, which leaves at 5 a.m. from Cuzco's San Pedro terminal (opposite the market) for the Macchu Picchu station. One way travel time is three to four hours.

The tourist train trip is best arranged by a local travel agency, which will charge up to $60 for the air-conditioned carriage to the Macchu Picchu station, bus transfer to the ruins, guided tour, lunch at the Hotel de Turistas and return journey by train and bus to Cuzco via Ollantaytambo. Fellow travellers will all be visiting tourists, mainly American. The coaches are locked in transit with no danger of having to mix with the local populace. The sacred valley of the Incas is seen through hermetically sealed windows.

The cheap and adventurous method is to take the local train, which leaves Cuzco at 5 a.m. daily. There are a variety of ticket classes available, including Pullman and first class. On the train it is hard to tell the difference: indeed, the adventure starts when trying to buy the ticket. The Cuzco station is one of the most dangerous places on the gringo trail for muggings, bag snatches and thefts. The single fare ($4) may be a lot cheaper than the tourist train, but this has to be weighed against the risk of being robbed while attempting to buy the cheaper ticket. On the local train itself, there are numerous reports of thefts in transit by locals who leap on and off at the switchbacks above Cuzco. This is why the tourist train travels with locked doors.

Finally, in order to board the local train, you have to walk the Cuzco streets at dawn and run the gauntlet to get into the station. The push and shove may only last 30 seconds, but it is unlikely that you will avoid an attempted theft. The best compromise of risk versus saving would seem to be to ask a trustworthy local, say a hotel employee, to buy the local priced ticket for you. The advantage of the local train is that it usually arrives earlier at the site, giving you more time before the hordes arrive.

Train times do vary, so all information should be checked on arrival in Cuzco. En route, after climbing the switchbacks from Cuzco, the train follows the course of the frothing Urubamba River down into lush montane forest. The best way to see Macchu Picchu without undue interference from other tourists is to try and stay overnight at the Hotel de Turistas (about $40). This will require booking well in advance, perhaps even from home. Accommodation at shorter notice can be obtained at nearby Aguas Calientes (about $7) in the valley below Macchu Picchu. Best by far is to walk the Inca Trail to Macchu Picchu, alighting from the train at Kilometre 88 and camping for three or four days along the way. Your arrival can be timed for dawn on the last day. As Macchu Picchu appears out of the mists you will see it much as the Incas did at the time of the Spanish conquest.

The Central Andean Line

El tren de la sierra climbs from sea level at Lima to 4783 m (15,700 ft) in the Ticlio–Galera tunnel beneath Mount Meiggs. Reached in 173 km (110 miles) from the coast, this is the highest tunnel and the highest standard gauge station, 4758 m (15,600 ft), in the world. Fifty kilometres (30 miles) beyond the summit the line descends to the Oroya junction at 3726 m (12,200 ft) having gone through 66 tunnels, crossed 59 bridges and negotiated 22 zigzags – all in seven hours.

The line was built at great expense, putting the Peruvian economy heavily in the debt of the USA as Peruvian guano was bartered for Oregon timber for the sleepers. If arriving from the coast, the traveller will receive the first sight of the Andes, llamas and the local campesinos. For scenery and railway buffs alike the ride is incomparable. Oxygen is produced on the Lima–La Oroya line to alleviate the effects of altitude sickness. It is possible to return to Lima from Oroya the same day – a five-hour taxi journey back.

From Oroya, the line branches north to Cerro de Pasco and south to Huancavelica, both rather desolate mining settlements. The southern branch passes the colourful Indian Sunday market of Huancayo. This is the end of the line, and whatever the map suggests, a dead end in terms of onward road travel to Cuzco. Some of the most beautiful scenery of the trip is to be seen between Oroya and Huancayo, passing the Javja valley. Railway enthusiasts might like to track down the last working Andes type 2-8-0 steam locomotive no 206, which is still in working order and rumoured to be locked in a shed in Huancayo.

Before the closure of the mine at Volcán the highest point of this line was formerly 4830 m (15,850 ft) on a siding off the La Cima line. Mount Meiggs was named after the American Henry Meiggs (1811–77), who engineered the line between 1867 and his death, after which work continued to completion in 1889.

The Southern Peruvian Line

This runs from Mollendo on the coast via Arequipa to Puna on Lake Titicaca and thence to Cuzco, reaching 4500 m (14,750 ft) at the Crucero Alto pass. There is no oxygen available on this line, so expect to bear the full brunt of altitude sickness if not acclimatized. Coca tea may help. The locked Pullman cars have heating, but otherwise the first- and second-class compartments are unheated, making blankets and warm clothes a necessity.

The Cuzco–Puno section is a favourite link on the gringo trail between Peru and Bolivia, climbing to 4267 m (14,000 ft) at La Raya, where snow peaks to 5500 m (18,000 ft) can be seen on both sides of the train, past the Altiplano town of Juliaca, famous for train bandits and thieves! From Puno a combination of boat, hydrofoil and bus completes the journey across Lake Titicaca to La Paz. On the map it may look like a feasible journey from Mollendo to Cuzco by train, but be warned – this could be a four-day epic, with overnight stops, for leather posteriors only!

Leaving Arequipa, the train slowly gains altitude, and it is three or so hours before the Altiplano is reached, a dry and empty prairie of tufted grass, punctuated by the occasional herd of vicuñas, llamas or their herdsmen. The volcanoes Misti (5822 m, 19,100 ft) and Nevado Chachani (6075 m, 19,900 ft) can be seen from the train, as can high altitude lakes (in particular Lago Lagunillas) home to large flocks of Andean flamingos. The bowler-hatted inhabitants of Canaguas give the first surprising clue that you have reached the Altiplano. Soon afterwards the spectacular rock formations of Sumbay will appear. Camping overnight here is the best way to explore the striated rocks, where 8000-year-old rock paintings adorn many of the caves.

BOLIVIA

The Chile–Bolivia, Arica–La Paz railway crosses the Atacama Desert, climbs to 4247 m (14,000 ft) at General Lagos arriving at La Paz after 444 km (278 miles) and some ten hours. Bolivian trains and railbeds are very old, poorly maintained and frequently shut down during the rainy season (December to April). Empresa National De Feroviarios (ENFE) is the national joke, and ENFE jokes are frequently employed as ways of passing the time while waiting to buy tickets and enduring delays. Dishevelled queues form days in advance to purchase tickets. Do not forget your passport since you will not be allowed to buy a ticket without one. As elsewhere in South America, first and second class are indistinguishable, and a third class – *bodegas*, or boxcars, resembling cattle wagons – are even cheaper. For the ultimate raw railroading experience locals sometimes even ride across the Altiplano on the roof of the train.

Best of the Bolivian bunch by far is the *ferrobus*, slightly more expensive, slightly more punctual and infinitely more pleasant than other Bolivian rolling stock. The La Paz–Arica connection was not operating at the time of writing. The Uyuñi–Pulcayo railway is Bolivia's oldest line, and runs on five ancient steam trains.

CHILE

The Antofagasta (Chile)–Bolivia railway (metre gauge) climbs to a summit of 3960 m (13,000 ft) at Ascolán. A Swiss engine pulls the train to Las Cuevas, in sight of Mt Aconcagua, in 12 hours. From Ollague a metre gauge spur once crossed a summit of 4826 m (15,800 ft) to the copper mines of Collahuasi, whence a 13 km (8 mile) aerial tram served the highest mine in the world on Aucanquilcha (about 6000 m,

home will stand you in good stead in the Andes. It is also a good opportunity to test out new boots, wear in your pack, and generally get in the swing of it. The best training for walking is walking.

EQUIPMENT

Boots

For an Andean trip, the best choice is a boot that can be worn for everyday travel. Ideally a lightweight trekking boot may be the answer. This will save on weight and duplication of kit. Vibram soles have good grip. Whatever you do decide upon, be sure to wear it in well before going. Gaiters can be useful for wet areas such as bogs or river crossings.

Clothes

It is not essential to spend very much on specialist gear. Track suits, woollen shirts and sweaters, wooly hats, and ski gloves are all useful. Avoid the flashier designer mountain

52. *Climbers walk to the Refugio Edward Whymper, at 5000 m (16,400 ft) on Chimborazo, Ecuador.*

clothing. Not only will you resemble a being from another planet to the average Andean *campesino*, but also if you are expensively dressed your chances of becoming a target for theft are much greater.

While Andean weather often requires only T-shirts and shorts, warm clothing is essential too. A combination of layers provides more insulation than one thick layer. Thermal underwear is made from a good combination of wool and synthetics that can cope with a variety of temperatures. It is also ideal for sleeping in when camping. One article that is perhaps worth investing in is a good set of waterproofs – I prefer breathables such as Gore–Tex – that should last some seasons, and provide an excellent top layer against the wind.

Shorts and swimming gear are essential, but note that it is considered strange to wear shorts

in urban areas, and even more so in country villages. '*Mire, un gringo sin pantalones*' ('Look, a gringo without trousers'), is a likely observation. Those wearing shorts in towns may well be greeted with a combination of suspicion, ridicule and disapproval. Jeans are almost useless for outdoor walking; they are heavy and chilling when wet and take a long time to dry. Preferable are modern lightweight 'travel trousers', such as Rohan.

Backpack

You will also need a comfortable pack, with good back support and shoulder straps, and preferably an adjustable waist band to place weight on your hips where it is more easily carried. An internal frame is best if the pack is to be used for general travel on buses. When travelling to South America, it may be worth placing your pack inside another bag that can be locked – it will also receive less damage in transit and protect the contents from dust when travelling on top of buses.

If a backpacking or trekking trip is the main

53. *Trekkers on the Inca Trail to Macchu Picchu, Peru.*

reason for your visit to the Andes, then you will only need to take what you need for the trek. Most visitors have other sights to see and a trek is only part of it, so try and double up on your walking and everyday travel gear. Above all, do not buy too big a pack. Total laden weight ideally should be under 10–12 kg (20–25 lb). Good makes in the UK are Karrimor and Berghaus, Lowe in the US.

Tent

A good tent or bivouac bag is essential, but can be quite expensive, especially if you are not planning to use it a great deal. However, once you have used a good tent it is unlikely you will want to use any other – it makes the difference between total comfort and total misery. A good lightweight tent should weigh under 2.5 kg (6 lb). Gore–Tex cuts down on condensation. Again this is an article that should be tested at home before travelling.

Sleeping bag

The same applies to a good sleeping bag. Modern synthetic bags are best. They stay warm even when wet, but tend to be very bulky and can easily occupy half of an average size pack. The more compact duckdown bags lose heat very quickly when wet. In the unpredictable Andes you may not be able to dry out a bag for days. A sleeping bag is also useful in the cheaper hotels to compensate for the lack of bedding in the cold nights. A light sleeping mat is essential for insulation and comfort when camping.

Stove and food

In some places it is possible to make a campfire out of locally gathered dead wood, whereas in others (e.g. national parks) it may be forbidden or impossible. In any event, a badly managed campfire can leave ugly scars. Many beautiful trekking areas, even Inca ruins, have been irreparably scarred in this way. At the altitudes encountered on most Andean walks, burned vegetation takes a long time to heal. Better and more reliable by far is to carry your own stove. Camping Gaz is good, but cannot be carried on aircraft because the canisters are pressurized. Better still is to take a petrol, paraffin or 'white gas' (meths or cooking fuel) stove, for which fuel is widely available locally. Some of the better makes combine stove and pans in one unit. Specially prepared freeze-dried camping meals are virtually unobtainable in South America, but many useful staples such as rice, dried fruit, nuts, etc. are obtainable at markets. To save time, take freeze-dried meals from home.

Storage while travelling

It is hard to find good quality camping, walking and climbing equipment in the Andes. Admittedly you can now hire most items from main centres, such as Cuzco and Huaras, but the quality is poor and boots are often not available

Other useful items

Essentials include a small pocket torch and slow-burning candles (to be used with caution in the tent); a Zippo all-weather lighter or 'Lifeboat' matches, which do not blow out; a penknife and a compass. A rudimentary medical kit should be carried for general travel, even when not backpacking.

in the larger sizes. Again, bring it from home. You will find a ready market should you wish to sell equipment at the end of your trip, and excess can easily be stored at a hotel when you are doing something else.

VENEZUELA

Varied scenery, excellent backpacking in cloud forest and retreating glacial terrain, cool clear Decembers ideal for making new routes on rock walls – these are the hallmarks of the Venezuelan mountains.

Sierra Nevada de Mérida

The area above Mérida is easily accessible from the city by what claims to be the highest cable car in the world, it goes in four stages to Pico Espejo (Mirror Peak) at 4765 m (15,633 ft). Walkers, even those who stroll from one cable car station to another, require a permit from the Oficina d'Inparque (Park Office), Avenida 4. For more extensive walks in the area a second permit must be obtained from the Defensa Civil (police), near the Estadio Santa Rosa. Permits are generally not given to single hikers.

November to May is the high tourist season for cable car trips and lift capacity is just 200 per hour, so if you plan to gain altitude the easy way, you may need to book ahead. January and February are particularly bad in this the most popular hiking area in the country. Early morning trips give the better views, but also attract the crowds. Note also that at peak times only two backpacks are allowed in each cable car. The cable car does not run every day and breakdowns are frequent. The best compromise is to take the cable car to the first station and begin the walk from there.

The Sierra Nevada de Merida is the only part of the Venezuelan Andes where snow lies permanently on the higher peaks at around 5000 m (16,400 ft). Inhabited villages are found at 800–1300 m (2500–4500 ft), and above this are found maize fields up to about 2000 m (6500 ft). Friendly locals can be seen in the fields, dressed in their colourful blue and red *ruanas* (local name for ponchos). Here is found the highest village in Venezuela – Los Nevados (2711 m, 8894 ft) – a four-hour walk from the Redonda cable car station. Another day trek is to the ice cave in the Timoncitos glacier.

From the summit station, the peaks known as the 'Five White Eagles' can be seen – Bolivar and its glacier (5007 m, 16,427 ft); Humboldt (4942 m, 16,213 ft); Bonpland (4882 m; 16,016 ft); Toro (4755 m, 15,600 ft); and León (4740 m, 15,551 ft). In the area there are a number of attractive lakes with good trout fishing – Laguna Negra in the Sierra Nevada National Park, Laguna Mcubaji, Lagunas Patos and Laguna La Canoa.

The high country is home to the *frailejón* (the 'great friar' plant, so much a symbol of the *paramos*, with some 40 local varieties), which blooms from September to December. Horseback treks can be made in the national park. El Camino Real (a four-hour trail) links the attractive villages of Apartaderos (where the Indian stone terraces are still ploughed by oxen) and Muchuchies. Puppies (a type of Grand Pyrenée) are sold at Sunday markets, where flower-selling and tourist-watching are favourite pastimes. Generally in the sierra keep a keen look out for hummingbirds as well as stray dogs. The Andean Club in Mérida organizes trips to the summits of the peaks, providing all guides and equipment.

COLOMBIA

The Sierra Nevada del Cocuy

This tropical, mist-shrouded range has been described as one of the most spectacular in the Andes, yet is comparatively unknown. Fifteen peaks over 5000 m (16,400 ft) dominate the western part of Colombia's Cordillera Oriental. The Guican–El Cocuy trek is quite accessible in this compact range (only 25 km, 16 miles long). Walking at an altitude of between 4000 m (13,100 ft) and 4600 m (15,100 ft) will be strenuous and requires experience, acclimatization and stamina. Parties must be self-sufficient on the five to six-day trek. There is no habitation on the way and the highest pass, which is in the middle of the trek, is guarded by a crevassed glacier. This involves the use of rope, ice axe and crampons for a safe traverse. Other than this there are no technical difficulties. The highest point seen on the walk is Ritacuba Blanco at 5330 m (17,487 ft). Other attractions are the flora, particularly the *frailejónes* and many attractive natural features, which merit the range's status as a national park. All types of weather can strike at any time, so adequate clothing and plenty of food is necessary. Maps can be obtained from the Instituto Geografico, Bogotá. It is normally dry from December to March, but January and February are the best months.

Los Nevados National Park

This park includes the highest volcanoes of Colombia's Cordillera Central, the best known being Nevado del Ruiz (5400 m, 17,716 ft) and Nevado del Tolima (5200 m, 17,060 ft). Nevado del Ruiz erupted in 1985 with catastrophic consequences. Rivers of mud, snow and rock destroyed the town of Armero, killing 20,000 people. The most popular access to the park, by jeep track to 4700 m (15,420 ft) near El Ruiz, is currently closed. Enquire at the Manzinales tourist office as to the situation. Altitudes in the park, from 2500 m (8200 ft) to the summits, encourage varied flora. In the southern part of the park you may see the Palma de Cela, Colombia's national tree, a palm that can grow 60 m (180 ft) tall.

Various one- or two-day treks can be made in the southern part of the park, to Laguna del Otun and Laguna la Leona. The most popular trek is to the summit of Nevado del Tolima, from El Silencio, accessible from Ibague to the south of the park. A tent is not essential for this two-day trek – there are some shelters *en route*. The last 300 m (1000 ft) or so is above the snowline. Crampons are needed but it is not technically difficult. January and February are considered the clearest months for walking.

Detailed descriptions of the above two treks can be found in Dydynski's *Colombia – a travel survival kit*.

ECUADOR

El Camino del Inca

This is one of the Inca trails, but not *the* Inca Trail. As mentioned elsewhere, the Incas were arguably the greatest footpath builders the world has known. This hike takes in a four- to six-day trip to Ingapirca, the best Inca site in Ecuador. Horses can be hired along part of the route. Although they may save your legs, horse trekking is no faster than on foot! Starting from Riobamba, travel to Alausi and then onwards by truck to Achupallas 3000 m (9840 ft), a small town with a *mestizo* combination of colourful Indians and Spanish colonial architecture.

The ancient Inca road is followed to campsites by the Lake of the Three Crosses and the ruins of Paredones. Side trips are available to the mystical Lake Culebrillas and to 'Labraschca Rumi', whence the stones were quarried to build Ingapirca. It is possible to camp near Ingapirca while exploring the ruins. At one stage the Inca road is as much as 7 m (25 ft)

wide, showing its former importance in Inca times. As Ingapirca comes nearer, the trail is less distinct across the moorland.

Ingapirca is no lost city. The Cañaris occupied the site for 600 years before the Incas arrived about 1490 after Huayna Capac conquered Ecuador. La Condamine mapped it in detail in 1739. The excellence of its stonework is comparable to that of Macchu Picchu, but the exact function of the Inca city is not known. It was probably a centre of sun worship as well as being a *Tambo* or inn for Inca messengers or travellers. From Ingapirca (3160 m, 10,367 ft) trucks leave regularly for the main road, the Pan American highway.

The Chimborazo trek

Chimborazo (6310 m, 20,703 ft) is Ecuador's highest peak, the 'Colossus of the Andes'. Fourteen glaciers have eroded its two craters into five summits. Ice from the glaciers is still sold in Indian markets. For the non-mountaineer who likes to walk, a circular trek is the ideal way to experience the high country and feel the presence of this mountain. One version of the trek starts from Poygos, with the first camp at Quedabra Colorado. From here the trek climbs to 4000 m (13,000 ft), descending to camp in the valley of Abraspungo, between Chimborazo and Carihuayrazo volcanoes. The next day's hike traverses the eastern slopes of Chimborazo, with good glacier views, to Chuquipogyo. Day four crosses the southern side of the mountain above the Riobamba valley to Totoras. The fifth day reaches the Refugio Edward Whymper at 5000 m (16,400 ft) at the foot of the Thielman glacier. The circuit to Poygos is completed via 'the great sand pit' (*arenal grande*), a vast desert at 4200 m (13,780 ft) on the western and north west slopes of Chimborazo. There are many variants of this hike, and the area is such that the well-equipped can make their own route round the mountain.

Hiking in the Cotopaxi area

The Cotopaxi National Park, established in 1975, is a microcosm of Andean highlife. Easily accessible by road from Quito to the north and Riobamba/Ambato to the south, a passable track leads to the park gates (entry US$10 for all foreigners). You are immediately rewarded by seeing a herd of semi-wild llamas and alpacas. The *paramo* lies between 3200 m (10,500 ft) and 4800 m (15,750 ft). Clear variations with altitude can be noted: the lower bog pasture around Lake Limpiopongo, then a level area of semi-desert, then barer pasture and finally the sandy wilderness (*arenal*) below the snowline and above the vegetation.

In this dramatic condor country, the summit of Cotopaxi is an obvious navigational aid. There are designated camping areas, as well as a mountain hut (Refugio José Ribas) at 4800 m (15,747 ft), sleeping 50. Only half an hour's walk from the end of the jeep trail, the hut is where most summit bids begin. A hike in the Cotopaxi park takes you round the highest active volcano in the world, in whose shadow you may be fortunate enough to see puma, deer, many types of bird, even a spectacled bear. On weekends the park road can be hitched, but during the week you must expect to walk most of the way from the main road to the park entrance, some 20 km (12 miles).

There are no set routes round the mountain, although Rachowieki (*Climbing and Hiking in Ecuador*) describes a route in detail. Allow about a week to circumnavigate the volcano at a comfortable pace and altitude. If acclimatized, a summit bid could be made from the hut in a long day (10–15 hours).

Baños and Tungurahua

Baños is a delightful town, gateway to the jungle and to the volcanoes, with access to one of Ecuador's easiest volcanoes (Tungurahua) as well as the more challenging El Altar massif. At a mere 1800 m (5905 ft) it can be a welcome respite from higher altitudes, with many pleasant low altitude walks in the area. It is too low for real acclimatization, so do not stay too long if you plan to trek or climb at altitude. Thermal baths and waterfalls are just some of the many attractions.

There are many more fabulous trekking areas in Ecuador, for instance the Sangay National Park, the largest wild area of Ecuador, with pumas and jaguar and every variety of natural habitat from the *paramo* at 5000 m (16,400 ft) to jungle at 1000 m (3200 ft). Sangay is the world's most active volcano. Even in sight of the capital, Quito, there are fine walks to the summits (4794 m, 5,728 ft) of the Pinchinchas, 10 km (6 miles) from the city centre.

See Rachowieki, *Climbing and Hiking in Ecuador*, for details.

PERU

Peru is well developed as a trekking centre. Guides cost about $15 a day, porters and mules about $5. It should be established whether they will bring their own food and shelter. It is not unknown for porters to arrive for a ten-day trek without food and equipped with just the clothes they stand up in – such as sandals for a trek involving scree and snow passes! Although Andean people are incredibly tough, checking their equipment prior to departure will make for a happier party.

The Huayhuash and Cordillera Blanca treks are both within eight hours of Lima, a mere hop by Andean standards. They have some of the most challenging hiking in the world, without the Himalayan factor of a long walk in to the start of the trek. In both cases, once you have crossed the first pass you had better be properly acclimatized. Commitment is essential for these treks. If you have a problem the only way out will be to climb back over the same pass or another pass of equal height. Best acclimatize by day walks in and around Huaras, trips to the Callejon de Huaylas, visits to the Puya Raimondii meadow, etc. These two ranges have the great advantage of relatively stable weather in their winter, roughly from May to August. Porters and mules can be hired at the park office in Huaras, which is also the best place to obtain maps. The most useful is *Trails of the Cordilleras Blanca and Huayhuash* by Jim Bartle, an American living in Huaras. The Cordilleras Huayhuash and Blanca were not colonized by the Incas to the same extent as the Cuzco area. Thus there are fewer ruins to see and those that are there, such as at Huantar de Chavin, are probably pre-Colombian. Organized treks to these areas can be made through Exodus. Their Alpamayo trek is especially spectacular.

The Cordillera Blanca

The Cordillera Blanca is an ideal choice for a quintessential Andean trek, with superb views, high altitude and open trails. Easily reached by road from Huaras, 400 km (250 miles) from Lima, it has a well trodden trek of five to six days. The Cordillera is almost completely contained in the Parque Nacional Huascaran, established in 1975. The range is some 180 km by 20 km (110 by 12 miles) in a park of 3365 sq km (1300 sq miles). Apart from containing Peru's highest peak (Huascaran 6768 m, 22,205 ft), this is the highest range in Peru and the highest anywhere in the world on the Equator. Thirty peaks exceed 6000 m (19,684 ft). Rivers, glacial lakes and eucalyptus groves are just some of the attractions, as well as the greatest concentration of glaciers on the equator. In the southern part of the park, although not on this hike, the famous *Puya raimondii* plant can be seen – in the Pachacoto valley. There is a US$3 entrance fee to the park.

As I write, the Cordillera Blanca trek and the Callejon de Huaylas are in an area designated by the Peruvian government as an emergency zone because of terrorist activities, principally of the Sendero Luminoso group. The British Foreign Office are also advising against travel to this area, close to Huaras, which achieved notoriety in 1989 for the murder of a tourist in a bomb attack on the town hall. Another incident involved the shooting of a 24-year-old Briton in Olleros. Tourists are not terrorist targets, but the terrorists are indiscriminate. However, this is one of the most spectacular treks in the Andes and one hopes it will be open again soon.

The highest passes on this trek are Punta Union and Portachuelo (4750 m, 15,600 ft). Huaras (3050 m, 10,006 ft) is the best town to pick up porters and mules and buy food, which is in short supply in the nearer Yungay. The altitude makes trekking the preferred option for this hike, and having only your camera to carry will make the trip infinitely more pleasant, and increase the chance of spotting condors and vicuñas along the way. Access by truck or *collectivo* to the start of the walk has been improved by a new road to the Lagunas Llanganucho, to the detriment of the first part of the hike.

The hike takes five to six days and rain, hail and snow can fall at any time, so good equipment is essential. The amount of climbing can be reduced by walking the route anti-clockwise. The normal route goes via Yungay, Lagos Llanganucos, Portachuelo, Colcabamba, Quedabra Paria, Punta Union, Quedabra Santa Cruz finishing at Cashapampa and Santa Cruz. The walking is not difficult – just the altitude – and is along wide open glacial valleys, across tufted grasslands, over scree passes and past azure glacial lakes with camping beneath awesome snowpeaks.

The Cordillera Huayhuash

Local expert Jim Bartle describes the trekking here as having '. . . no real highlights, just a long series of overwhelming views'. Only 50 km (30 miles) from the Huascaran Park lies the Cordillera Huayhuash, a smaller and more self-contained ridge only 30 km (20 miles) north to south, containing equally spectacular peaks and some of the world's most challenging high mountain climbs, including Peru's second peak, Yerupaja at 6634 m (21,766 ft).

Extensive treks can be made here. A favourite is the 160 km (100 miles) circular trek that takes 10–15 days. Rugged and only for fit, acclimatized, committed trekkers, the Huayhuash is remote. It is two day's walk from the road before the trek even begins, at the town of Chiquian.

At least one good high altitude trek should have been made before attempting this one. The highest point is Punta Cuyoc 5000 m (16,400 ft) and the trail, which stays high but undulating through most of its length, begins and ends at Chiquian (3400 m, 11,150 ft). Access is via Huaras.

The Ausangate hike

Close to Cuzco, the high open country of the Ausangate hike presents a strong contrast to the enclosed jungle paths of the Inca Trail. The circular trek takes four to seven days, passing a number of snow peaks, close to crumbling glaciers and lakes, past herds of alpacas and llamas, ice caves and hot springs.

Viscachas, caracaras, Andean geese, and giant coots are just some of the wildlife that may be encountered. Walkers will see local weaving and pass by the small *campesino* villages of Ocongate and Tinqui, where mules and porters can be hired. Buy all food and provisions in Cuzco.

The highest point on this trek is Punta Ausangate (4900 m, 16,075 ft) so again acclimatization is a must. The trek can be made from Ocongate or Pitumarca, with reasonably easy access from Cuzco. See *Apus and Incas* (Brod) and *Trekking in Peru and Bolivia* (Bradt) for detailed routes on this trek. The South American Explorers Club produce the best map.

The Inca Trail

The Inca Trail is the hike that has everything, encapsulating the Andean experience in a nutshell. As well as altitude (the highest pass is 4200 m, 13,779 ft) the trail has staggering views of montane forest, permanent snow peaks Salcantay and Veronica, hummingbirds and mossy but intact Inca ruins connected by pathways along precipitous ridges. It was built by the Incas as part of the longest footpath network in the world, some 5200 km (3250 miles) from Pasto in Colombia to Tucuman in Chile.

Essentially, this is a mountainous jungle walk, in contrast to the open trekking of other parts of the Andes. Though fairly strenuous, it is not too difficult for the average acclimatized walker. After three to five days of magnificent scenery, camping in or near Inca ruins, the Gateway of the Sun is reached. Below, if the dawn and the clouds are kind, stretches out the lost city of the Incas, Macchu Picchu. Never found by the Spaniards, it was only 'rediscovered' by the explorer Hiram Bingham in 1911. After centuries of neglect (although not to local people), parts of the trail were found in Bingham in 1915. Later explorations in 1942 by Paul Fejos and again in 1968 by Victor Angeles enabled the 'trail' to be identified and further opened. Since then it has become the most popular trail in South America, with upwards of 8000 hikers every year.

May to September are the driest months to walk the trail, but unfortunately more crowded. The rest of the year – the rainy season – is quieter, but it really is wet. The trail is slippery and quite dangerous in places. Most walkers start the trail from the point known as Kilometre 88 of the local train from Cuzco to Macchu Picchu. Be ready to get off since the train only stops for a moment.

You now cross the river by a new bridge. Only a short while ago this was a formidable obstacle. An elderly local, whose family owned much of the land over which the trail runs, demolished the existing bridge. He operated an

oroya, a steel cable with a pulley and a basket, and charged walkers to be pulled across. Now with the new bridge it costs $12 to enter the 'park' and off you go, climbing through eucalyptus groves to the first official campsite and the ruins of Llactapacta. The terraces are good examples of the efficiency of Inca agriculture. Close by Kilometre 88 is the Cusich-acha project, which has the joint aim of archae-ological research and land rehabilitation, aiming to restore the productivity of Inca times.

After three or so hours the only village on the trail, Huayllabamba, is reached at 3000 m (9800 ft). Three hours more, through steepening woods and increasingly spectacular terrain, gains the treeline and a meadow, Llulluch-apampa, at 3680 m (12,073 ft). This is the last campsite before the first and highest pass (Abra de Huarmihuañusca – 'Dead woman's pass') at 4198 m (13,772 ft). From the pass the ruins of Runcurucay may be seen, dominating the valley. It really feels like walking in the steps of the Incas, towards the second pass, Abre de Runcurucay, 3998 m (13,116 ft). The Inca feel stays with the walker now on the Inca steps leading to the secret city of Sayacmarca. Two hours beyond Sayacmarca you reach the fasci-nating ruins of Phuyupatamarca, where clear water cascades through the remains of five Inca stone baths. The name means 'cloud level town'. From the nearby campsite, superb views of snowpeaks Salcantay, Pumasillo and Veronica, all around 6000 m (19,500 ft) can be had. Note though that although water is plentiful on the trail it should always be sterilized.

From here a 'new' section of the trail has been opened up. It is in fact the original stone staircase of more than 1000 steps down to Huinay Huayna through an Inca tunnel. In a section scarred by powerlines, a new 'tourist hotel' has been built, where walkers can sleep for under $3 per night. The ruins here are the most extensive on the trail so far. The hotel is also conveniently placed for the pre-dawn walk to Intipunku, the Gate of the Sun, which overlooks Macchu Picchu and the end of the trail. Plan to reach Macchu Picchu before the tourist train arrives, and you will get the best possible feel of this spectacular city that has captured the imagination of every visitor. When it becomes busy, leave your pack at the *guarderia* and take the final hike up to Huayna Picchu. The reward, after a further hour's hike, is a magnificent view of the lost city, crowning the Macchu Picchu experience.

After this you have three choices; hope for a cancellation at the almost certainly overbooked hotel, return by train to Cuzco, or walk down to Aguas Calientes, a small village by the Macchu Picchu railway station. Here there are a couple of rudimentary guest houses and thermal baths to ease aching limbs.

The popularity of the Inca Trail is threatening its magnificence. As long ago as 1980, litter and erosion were identified as the most obvious threats to the trail, and an expedition specially organized to clear it up collected 300 kg (700 lb) of rubbish. In 1985, another expedition collected double that amount. The problem is not helped by the fact that many travellers on the Inca Trail have no hiking experience. They are unfamiliar with the concepts of taking away litter and carefully choosing campsites and taking care with fires so as to minimize their impact on the trail and the local community. Since the train to Kilometre 88 has become such an attraction to travellers to South America, it has also become popular with professional gangs of thieves. Robbery has now spread to the trail itself, and travellers are advised not to walk the trail in groups of less than six. In 1988 a Dutch couple went missing, believed murdered, on the trail.

Despite these reservations, walking the trail is a great deal of fun. You can imagine you have trodden in Inca footsteps, through fields of orchids, camping in their ruins by moonlight.

54. An Inca footpath above Pisaq, Peru.

One needs little imagination to feel an Inca presence above the roar of the Urubamba River. Clouds unfold views of ceaseless novelty while snowpeaks intermittently crystallize above the montane forest.

Other paths may confuse route-finding in many places, and it is very possible to get lost along the way. Maps are available in Cuzco and it is also well worth consulting some of the main walking guides, such as Bradt, Frost, Brod, etc. It is also possible to hire guides and porters in Cuzco, although this might take away some of the feeling of doing it yourself. Remember that this is a mountain walk and can be very wet and cold at times. Pay close attention to the suitability of your equipment before departing.

55. Inca terraces from the trail above Pisaq, Peru.

Essential reading for trekkers in Peru includes: *Apus and Incas* by Charles Brod; *Exploring Cusco* by Peter Frost, Nuevas Imagenes; *Backpacking in Peru and Bolivia*, Hilary Bradt, Bradt Publications.

BOLIVIA

Bolivian routes are less frequented than the Peruvian classics. Mules are generally less available than in Peru, so there is less trekking and more backpacking. Although many walks are confined to high ground, some of the best in the Cordillera Real, close to La Paz, involve one high pass early on and then descend gently to much lower altitudes in the Yungas jungle region. This makes for an interesting variant on the high, cold walks of Peru. These trails will gain popularity if Peru's best areas remain out of bounds because of terrorism.

The Cordillera Real and the Takesi trail

The Cordillera Real is easily reached by public transport from La Paz, and contains a number of interesting hikes through a region with views of five peaks over 6000 m (19,684 ft) and many over 5000 m (16,400 ft). The Takesi trail takes two to three days and will appeal to acclimatized walkers with little experience. Maps are hardly needed, so well signposted is the route. Much of it is a wide paved pre-Inca trail that tempers the climb to the first pass at 4650 m (15,256 ft) by shallow steps. From here the trail winds slowly down towards the Yungas and terminates at Chojlla at 2100 m (6900 ft).

There are many other walks in the Cordillera Real, such as the La Cumbre to Coroico hike (the Choro trail), which again starts high (4850 m, 15,912 ft) and descends into the humid Yungas (1000 m, 3300 ft), four days hike, again along pre-Inca footpaths. The return trip from La Cumbre to La Paz by bus or *collectivo* takes just an hour – a spectacular trip of 96 km (55 miles). The Zongo to La Cumbre or Coroico routes link with other hikes, giving high and low altitude choices, with excellent views of the glaciers of Huayna Potosi (6088 m, 19,973 ft).

A rugged but varied trek of from three to seven days can be made in the Illimani area, Bolivia's highest mountain (6480 m, 21,259 ft). This also ends up in the jungle, starting at 4700 m (15,419 ft) and descending to Chulumani (1800 m, 5905 ft). The shores of Lake Titicaca also have some excellent hikes, notably, with the assistance of a boat, to the Island of the Sun.

See Bradt's *Backpacking and Hiking in Peru and Bolivia* for more details.

CHILE AND ARGENTINA

The Chilean/Argentinian Lake District

The lake district covers an area about 300 by 160 km (200 by 100 miles) north-east of Puerto Montt in Chile, split about equally between Chile and Argentina. On the Chilean side the lakes are quite low, around 300 m (1000 ft) up and the climate is mild. The Argentine lakes tend to lie between 600 and 1700 m (1950 and 5500 ft), in an altogether cooler and wilder terrain. This is a varied and interesting area for backpacking, without acclimatization problems. Local people in this sparsely populated district are a convivial mixture of Indians, *gauchos, estancieros* and immigrants from Europe – many of them German or Swiss. Valdivia and Puerto Montt have a particularly expatriate feel about them, and this European feel is echoed by the decidedly alpine character of this part of the Andes.

Argentine San Carlos de Bariloche doubles as a glamour resort for skiers, hikers and fur-coated chocolate munchers by summer and winter. Trains from Santiago de Chile take 15 hours overnight to Valdivia and 20 hours to Puerto Montt. From Buenos Aires on the Argentine side, a 32-hour train trip will take you to Bariloche. The best views are in the last four hours. Those with less time on their hands will find the two-hour flight from Buenos Aires more convenient.

The choice of hikes is myriad. One of the remotest and finest walks starts from Quillén, at the entrance to the Lanin National Park in Argentina. Views of the Lanin and Llaima volcanoes wind through monkey puzzle groves with the chance to see varied flora and fauna. The walk takes three to five days and is best done between December and March. Pleasant day walks can be had to Cerro Chapelco from San Martin de los Andes (also giving good volcano views) and around Osorno above Lake Llanquihue.

Some of the finest medium-altitude Andean hiking can be had on the Chile–Argentina hike from Lake de Todos Los Santos to Lake Mascardi. This is also covered by a 200 km (125 mile) tourist route that combines buses and boats. The best scenery is seen in three day's easy walking, about 50 km (30 miles), from Lake de Todo los Santos to Pampa Linda. Here time can be saved by hitching a lift, since the best scenery is now behind you.

One of the most rugged and spectacular lake district walks is the three-day Cerro Catedral circuit along waymarked trails from Bariloche, with well placed and maintained *refugios* along the way, dispensing with the need for tents. November to May is the best hiking season. This is not a beginner's walk as it is not completely waymarked and contains some fairly arduous scrambling.

Wilder still is the Lago Mascardi to Lago Negra walk, which in clear weather can give views of Mount Tronador and as far as Volcan Osorno into Chile. This again is not for beginners, but traverses some of the least spoiled country in Argentina in about five days.

Torres del Paine

The Paine Horns (Cuernos De Paine) National Park has some of the finest backpacking country in the world, assuming the often inclement weather is kind enough to part the clouds. Paine may have been an early woman explorer or an Indian word for blue, but the park acquired its new name in 1959 after being previously called Parque National del Grey. More recently a 25,000 acre sheep pasture has been added to the park. The impressive Cerro Paine (3050 m, 10,006 ft) has one of the highest rock walls in the world. The sheer east face of 1200 m (3936 ft) was first climbed by South Africans in 1974.

You might see guanacos, red and grey foxes, Andean flamingoes and condors; you will certainly see spectacular scenery and the awesome Grey glacier, calving icebergs 150 feet (40 m) into the water. The tourist season here runs from December to February, the southern Chilean summer. Outside this peak season, it may be difficult to find transport to the park from Puerto Natales, but the park office in town can be helpful. In season, buses run most days, taking four hours from Puerto Natales to the Park Administration centre, making the park accessible even just for a day trip. For keen walkers there are weeks of trails.

The most popular hike is the three- or four-day return trip to Lago and Glaciar Grey. Rather more arduous is the eight-day hike around the whole massif via Lagos Grey, Dickson and Paine. Other excellent walks are to Laguna Verde (two to three days there and back), Lago Pingo (two days each way) and Refugio Paine (five days there and back). There are myriad variations.

The best local map is published by the Corporación Nacional Forestal (CONAF) and is available at the park entrance. It marks all the roads, trails, and refugios. Check on the feasibility of your route before committing yourself – conditions do change. Another good map is that produced by Eduardo Scott, c/o Restaurant Rio Serrano, Puerto Natales. Within the park there are two hotels – the Pehoe, with beautiful views across the lake to the Paine towers, and the Posada Rio Serrana, on the road to Lago Grey. Eduardo Scott, the producer of the map, is also a recommended local guide for the Paine region and organizes tours from day trips to long treks.

A pleasant surprise in the park is the presence of carefully marked hiking trails, some 250 km (150 miles) long, signposted with red and orange flashes. Less pleasant is the effect that such easy access has had on the park. Some refugios have been vandalized for firewood, in singular disregard for the comfort and safety of others. Such selfishness is all the more infuriating when it is found seemingly at the end of the earth. Because of this, and because the *refugios* tend to get crowded in peak season, a tent is infinitely better.

Journey Latin America and Exodus do specialist trips to the Patagonian Andes – Fitzroy and Paine.

Los Glaciares National Park – Argentina

One of the great mountain experiences in the Andes, or indeed anywhere in the world, is the Los Glaciares National Park. It combines the spectacular ever-calving glaciers of Perito Moreno and Upsala (just two of 300 glaciers) with the dramatic spires of Mount Fitzroy and Cerro Torre. Extreme climber, hiker, seeker of rare flora and fauna, photographer or glacier watcher – there is something here for every lover of wild places in the 6000 sq km (2300 sq mile) park. A US$40 helicopter ride above the Perito Moreno gives an unusual perspective of the size of these rivers of ice.

The small town of Calafate on Lago Argentina is the base for exploring the park, best reached from Ushaia in the south by military flight on LADE. From Chile, there are buses along the 330 km (200 miles) of desert track that separates these two southern outposts of civilization. Be sure to book your trip out of Calafate, since routes are busy in high season. Calafate is a frontier town with frontier prices (cash dollars only).

The Perito Moreno glacier is unique in being one of the few glaciers in the world that is still growing. It is also, at 450 m (1500 ft) a year, a very fast moving glacier. Named after a nineteenth-century Argentine explorer, its main feature is the 5 km (3 mile) wide snout. Sixty metre (200 ft) ice towers collapse into the lake creating impressive waves. Beware of standing too near the lake at any time of year, since the enormous waves have been known to wash unsuspecting tourists off their chosen perch.

Every three or four years the ice advances across the narrow centre of the Brazo Rico and closes the Canal de los Tempanos (Channel of the Icebergs), cutting off the upper part of the lake. The water rises some 30 m (70 ft). Eventually the pressure bursts the dam and the result is a spectacular surge of water and ice. Daytrips to see this can be arranged from Calafate, but the savagery of the scene is considerably diluted by the presence of large numbers of other tourists. It is recommended to camp in the area for maximum enjoyment. Similar trips can be arranged to the Upsala glacier, and the Agassiz, Bolado, Onelli and Spegazzini glaciers.

Cerro Fitzroy

The Fitzroy range lies on the northwest shores of Lago Viedma. At least five days are needed for a good hike in this area. However, it is possible to get a glimpse of the peaks, if you are lucky, in a daytrip from Calafate, five hours and 240 km (150 miles) from town. December to March is the best time to visit. Buy a map at the park office in town before leaving. Within the park there are two basic hostels, at Lago Desierto and Lago Viedma. To do the three main walks, to Fitzroy, to Cerro Torre and to Lago Toro would require five to six days for the round trip. Views of Cerro Torre can be elusive because of the severe weather at most times of year.

The best currently available guide to hiking in this region is the Bradt publication *Backpacking in Chile and Argentina*, which has detailed descriptions of ten superb walks in the lake district and Patagonia, as well as other parts of Argentina and Chile.

CHAPTER 10 Climbing

HISTORY

Long before Mont Blanc was conquered the less superstitious local Indians had climbed a number of high Andean summits for use as lookouts or to make offerings to spirits. Inca relics have been found on some of the easier volcanic peaks around the Altiplano and Puna de Atacama. Here even high peaks may be below the 5800 m (19,000 ft) snowline and no technical equipment would be necessary. The concept of mountaineering for sport (*Andinismo*) lagged far behind Europe and the 'golden age' of Alpine mountaineering. After the Spanish conquest there was little interest in the high Andean peaks, the *conquistadores* being more involved with the search for Inca gold.

Archaeological evidence supports this. In 1954 a mummy was unearthed on Cerro Plomo. In 1964 the frozen corpse of an Indian dressed in a cloak, with a rope, a catapult and leather shoes was found on Cerro del Toro (6386 m, 20,951 ft). He had been sacrificed. Aconcagua, highest peak in the Andes (6960 m, 22,834 ft) fell in 1897 to the Fitzgerald/Zurbriggen party, but the discovery of a frozen guanaco above 6300 m (20,700 ft) raises the question of whether the summit may have been attained long before Fitzgerald's accredited climb. There is evidence that the Atacama Indians ascended Llullaico (6723 m, 22,056 ft), which was for a while the highest known human ascent until the Schlaginweits reached 6785 m (22,260 ft) on Abi-Gamin in 1855. Although the Indians may have conquered some summits in the course of their everyday lives, climbing for the sake of it really relied on the visitors. Only then was true *Andinismo* born.

Foreign interest in the mountains of the Equator was given impetus by the eighteenth-century discussion about whether the world was a neat sphere or whether it was flattened at the poles. The French scientist La Condamine visited Ecuador between 1736 and 1744, during which time he measured the height of Chimborazo at 6310 m (20,702 ft), although he only reached about 4750 m (15,500 ft). Chimborazo was then believed to be the highest in the world, a claim that still has some justification, since with the now established equatorial bulge, we know that it is the furthest peak from the centre of the earth. Of course many peaks are higher above sea level, which is the normal method of defining altitude. After spending 28 days at altitude on Corazon, La Condamine started his journey home by travelling 3000 km (2000 miles) down the Amazon to Cayenne on the Atlantic coast. Like many of his contemporary travellers, he was no shirker.

In 1802 the German explorer Humboldt made various attempts on Chimborazo, reaching 5875 m (19,274 ft), and he died happy in the knowledge that this was the highest altitude ever reached by Western man. His record was topped by the Frenchman Boussingault in 1831 at 6000 m (19,684 ft). Various expeditions of little note took place in the mid 1800s, and the breakthrough, in terms of mountaineering achievement, came in 1872 when the German Reiss and the Colombian Escobar reached the summit of Cotopaxi 5897 m (19,346 ft). Reiss and Stübel climbed Tungurahua (5016 m, 16,456 ft) the next year.

1880 saw the spectacular campaign of Edward Whymper, of Matterhorn fame. Allied with his former Matterhorn adversary Carrell he climbed Cotopaxi (fifth ascent) and made first ascents of Chimborazo, Cayambe, Antisana, Illinza Sur, Carihuairazo and a number of other notable peaks. Of the major peaks only El Altar, whose summit remained unconquered until 1963, eluded the Whymper party. To this day it remains one of the most technically challenging Ecuadorian peaks. Whymper left his mark not only on the annals of Andean climbing, but also on a street in the Ecuadorean capital, Quito, as well as the new Refugio Whymper, at 5000 m (16,400 ft) on the slopes of Chimborazo. Then, as now, politics intervened to thwart Whymper's original aim to climb in the very highest Andean regions of Chile, Bolivia and Peru, who were at war. Who knows what else he may have achieved had these peaks been accessible?

The modern era has seen a new interest by Ecuadorian mountaineers in their own mountains, and great importance has been attached to mountaineering as a magnet for tourists who wish to savour the combined attractions of equatorial volcanic peaks in a still relatively stable political climate.

In Peru, the summit of Huascaran Norte was claimed by Anne Peck in 1908, while many summits of the Cordillera Blanca fell to German or Austrian expeditions in the 1930s. Summits in the other main Peruvian cordilleras (Huayhuash, Vilcabamba, Urubamba and Vilcanota) were reached after World War II. In southern Peru, Hiram Bingham's 1911 Macchu Picchu party reached the summit of Coropuna (6613 m, 21,696 ft) with mixed emotions. 'While we were all glad to reach the top', he confided, 'we were all agreed we would never do it again.' El Misti

56. Chimborazo, Ecuador.

volcano (5842 m, 19,166 ft) was first officially climbed on a mule, but local Indians had almost certainly been there before. In Bolivia, Illimani was first climbed by a British party in 1898.

The two main ranges of the Patagonian ice-cap were explored much later, partly because of their inaccessibility. In the Northern Patagonian ice cap, the highest peak (Cerro San Valentin, 4058 m, 13,313 ft) was first climbed in 1952 by an Argentinian expedition, while the most interesting peak in the region, Cerro Fitzroy (3375 m, 11,072 ft) was claimed by the Italians Magnone and Terry in the same year. The nearby bastion of Cerro Torre (3128 m, 10,262 ft) was not climbed until 1977 by Maestri and Egger, while the central tower of the Paine massif, Cerro Paine (3050 m, 10,006 ft) was first ascended in 1974 by a South African party.

CLIMBING TODAY

A general look at the geography and history of the Andes quickly establishes that climbing in the Andes can match any challenge that high-altitude climbing in the Alps offers, with the addition of extreme altitudes only really otherwise encountered in the Himalayas. Despite their height, access to many of the climbs is much quicker than in the Himalayas, where long treks to base camp are the norm.

> Scan the introduction to the Andean trekking chapter and you will see that most equipment needs to be brought from home. In terms of high-altitude climbing hardwear, this is even more the case. Any major climb has to be regarded as a self-supporting expedition. There are a number of good local guides to the major peaks, and the hire of mules and porters may assist the party to arrive at a base camp in relatively good shape. Remember that in the Andes there is no organized rescue network such as in the Alps or North America, and that in case of an accident or emergency, the party will have to rely on itself for rescue.

Despite the altitude, not all of the highest peaks are technically difficult; some might even be described as 'trekking peaks'. But because of the altitude and self-reliance factor, the Andean peaks are no place to learn the rudiments of high-altitude mountaineering – experience must be gained in advance, even if you plan to join a professionally guided party. You may hear stories of travellers reaching the summit of lower peaks such as Tungurahua in shorts and gym shoes, and these stories are probably true, but such ascents are a fluke, and fatalities are not infrequent in Andean mountaineering.

For some background reading of how even experienced mountaineers can fare in the Andes, Joe Simpson's *Touching the Void* is essential reading. It is the true story of disaster and survival by two climbers on Siula Grande (6344 m, 20,813 ft) in Peru's Cordillera Huayhuash. Climber or not, this is one of the most exciting reads, fact or fiction, you are likely to encounter. Fortunately, not all climbing expeditions to the Andes have such an epic outcome.

If you already have some Alpine mountaineering experience, then there is no reason why you should not, with the appropriate acclimatization, attempt some of the more famous peaks in the Andes with a balanced and perhaps guided party. If you do not already have this experience, the only advice I have is 'go and get it', before you try the Andes.

There follows a description of some of the more famous Andean peaks, famous either because of their height, their propensity to erupt, their place in the history of *Andinismo*, or because of their climbing challenge. This is a personal choice – thousands of others could equally well fill their place. The only other small detail to bear in mind is that in the Andes, south faces are the equivalent of north faces, since in the southern hemisphere it is the south face of a mountain that rarely sees the sun.

CHIMBORAZO, Ecuador (6310 m, 21,702 ft)
Simón Bolívar dubbed this 'The watch tower of the Universe'. Chimborazo is of old volcanic origin. It is named for the God of the Puruhás, later adored by the Incas. The Quechua word *Chimbo* means the other side, *Rassu* means snow. In Inca mythology Chimborazo was the husband of Tungurahua and they were united in severe storms. Long believed to be the highest peak on earth, Chimborazo's equatorial location attracted eighteenth-century scientists keen to measure the circumference of the earth and to establish whether the earth was a true sphere or whether it flattened at the poles.

Chimborazo is actually further from the centre of the earth than Mount Everest, and the point on earth that is nearest to the sun. La Condamine and Humboldt made the most famous failed attempts to climb it. Chimborazo was first climbed by Whymper on 4 January 1880 with the Italian guide brothers Carrell, by what is now known as the Whymper route. When doubt was cast on their achievement – Chimborazo was long thought unclimbable – they repeated the ascent six months later via Pogyos in the company of two Ecuadorians.

Prior acclimatization (at least a week) is recommended before attempting Chimborazo. Although not technically difficult, ice and wind slab avalanche danger are prominent factors. Any time of year is possible, but opinions vary as to the best time. December can be clear, June and July also. April often brings heavy snow. October and November can be wet and windy. Many ascents have been recorded in January and February. In a nutshell, go any time and be prepared for anything.

The old route is the original Whymper first ascent route, the new route is the one taken the second time via Pogyos. The Pogyos route is less used today, although it was formerly considered easier than the Whymper route. At Pogyos (4000 m, 13,123 ft) it is possible to hire mules to go to the Zurita refuge. Really a tent is preferable – the refuge is in poor repair and sleeps 15 in squalor. The route is losing its appeal as the glacier has receded, leaving an awkward band of scree at around 5000 m (16,400 ft).

More popular is the route via the Whymper refuge, which is reached by a 20 km (12 mile) track via the Ambato–Guaranda highway. It is best to make private travel arrangements (e.g. taxi) to the end of the road at 4800 m (15,747 ft) where accommodation and cooking facilities are available in the new hut. Just prior to the ascent, walk to the upper Whymper refuge at 5000 m (16,400 ft) for an early start.

The normal route leaves the hut at midnight.

57. *Chimborazo, Ecuador 6310 m (20,703 ft) and the Refugio Edward Whymper.*

A fit acclimatized party should reach the summit in eight or nine hours, returning to the hut the same day. Snow level is about the same as the upper hut at about 5000 m (16,400 ft). The classic route has substantial danger from falling seracs, ice towers on the glacier. Many prefer the slightly more technical variation of the classic Whymper route. This goes fairly directly up the Thielmann glacier above the hut, right to about 5800 m (19,000 ft), when it forks left to the skyline (the Arista de Nieve) and seracs at about 6000 m (19,700 ft), then along the skyline (as seen from the hut) to the summit.

There are many variants, via the Agujas de Chamonix and the Corridor, to name but two. Other summits, which provide more challenging climbs than the Whymper summit are the Veintimilla (6267 m, 20,561 ft); the north summit at 6200 m (20,341 ft); the Politecnica (6000 m, 19,685 ft) and the Martinez summit (5500 m, 18,044 ft). Chimborazo still has a number of new routes yet to be made, as well as many known routes with only one or two prior ascents.

COTOPAXI, Ecuador (5897 m, 347 ft)

This is the highest active volcano in the world, dominating the Tiopullo range, with a circular base of some 20 km (12 miles). Although not particularly active in recent years, previous eruptions have caused great concern in the towns and valleys of Latacunga, Los Chillos and even as far away as Quito. In one of its greatest early eruptions a 200-ton block was hurled 16 km (10 miles), ash clouds settled up to 300 km (200 miles) away and the noise was heard 800 km (500 miles) distant.

Unusually for a volcano, it erupts only from one cone. We know of one eruption in 1534 during a decisive battle between the Spanish and the Indians. The Spanish had never heard an eruption, while the Indians considered it an example of divine wrath. One of the worst modern eruptions was in 1977, when melted glaciers crashed into the valleys, devastating cities all the way to the Pacific 250 km (150 miles) away. Cotopaxi is one of the few Ecuadorean peaks that Whymper did not claim as a first ascent – the German Reiss and Colombian Escobar got there first in 1872. Whymper's second ascent route now bears the stamp of the 'normal' route.

Cotopaxi lies at the centre of its own national park, to which access has been considerably improved in recent years. No official transport goes into the park but hitchhiking from the Panamerican highway is possible at weekends. For a small group a taxi or private hire is quickest. The José Ribas hut, built in 1971 by the mountaineering club of San Gabriel school, is the obvious base for the climb, at 4800 m (15,748 ft) it is just around the snowline. A guardian provides gas for cooking, water, 50 bunks and even occasional electricity in the hut, which is open all year. The access road to 4600 m (15,091 ft) is a half-hour walk from the end of the jeep track.

Two main summit routes from the hut are possible, though one is occasionally barred by a difficult crevasse. The old route takes about eight hours via the glacier. Climbers leave at midnight to gain the benefit of the hardest snow, with stronger crevasse bridges and less chance of avalanche. Cotopaxi's glaciers, as elsewhere, are retreating.

The dawn approach to the crater is accompanied by a strong smell of sulphur. The crater rim has a number of points of nearly equal altitude, and so it is arguable that the actual summit may not have been reached until the 1950s. Dawn is often the clearest time on the summit – some 20 major peaks can be seen. The bottom of the crater gapes some 800 m (2600 ft) below the rim. Cotopaxi is currently in one of its dormant phases and only a few sulphurous fumaroles mark the cannon barrel crater that shot hot lava, ice and mud 250 km (150 miles) to the ocean in the great eruption of 1877.

EL ALTAR, Ecuador (5319 m, 17,451 ft)

Called 'Capac Urcu (Sublime mountain)', by the Incas, the name Altar was coined by the Spanish *conquistadores*, who wanted to clothe it with religious significance. They gave religious names, such as Bishop and Acolyte, to its various other peaks according to their position and standing.

El Altar is reached most easily from Riobamba, thence to Penipe, Hacienda Releche and the Collanes camp. El Altar's position – facing

the Amazon jungle – puts it in one of the wettest areas of the country, resulting in magnificent glaciers and ice formations, which are constantly avalanching. The peaks of the Altar form a semi-circle, opening towards the west. November to February are generally considered to be the best times for successful ascents. Surrounding the Altar are vast untouched areas of *paramos* where deer, bear and condor can be seen. There are also Indian villages and old farms.

El Obispo (the Bishop), is the highest point on the Caldera (the 'cauldron' or 'cooking kettle') rim and was reached in July 1963 by Tremonti's Italian party. A lower point on the rim was reached in 1939. One of the few to have escaped the successes of Whymper, this was the last 5000 m (16,400 ft) peak in Ecuador to be climbed. El Canonigo (the Canon) is to

58. *The* caldera *of El Altar's summits (5319 m – 17,452 ft), seen from Riobamba, Ecuador.*

the north of the Cauldron, with hanging glaciers. The third in altitude is La Monja Grande (the Mother Superior), a rock needle crusted with ashes and ice. Los Frailes (the Three Friars) have white hoods of snow drooping towards the cauldron. El Tabernaculo (the Tabernacle) and the Acolito (the Acolyte) are other peaks on the rim.

The Obispo climb takes two to three days with a bivouac from the Collanes site. It is the most frequently climbed of Altar's peaks, and easier than Canonigo and the northern peaks. The latter are usually attempted from a base camp at Cerro Negro, accessible from Collanes, with a camp at Cerro Negro and a bivouac on the route. The Friars are also accessible from here, and would be well worth the climb for novelty value – they have very few recorded ascents.

HUASCARAN, Peru (6768 m, 22,205 ft)

Huascaran is Peru's highest peak, situated in the Cordillera Blanca, near Huaras, some eight hours from the capital, Lima. The north peak summit, Huascaran Norte (6655 m, 21,834 ft) was the subject of a disputed claim by Miss Anne Peck in September 1908, together with Swiss guides Taugwalder and Zumtaugwald, both of whom suffered badly from altitude sickness. The summit claim has not been completely discounted and would then have been the women's altitude record, which Peck was hoping to win from the delicately named Fanny Bullock Workman. The determined Anne Peck earned the title 'The Lady of Huascaran'.

The higher peak Huascaran Sur was first ascended in July 1932 by an Austrian party; Phillippe Borchers, Erwin Schneider, Hans Kinzl, Bernhardt, Hoerlin and Hein. The same party made many other first ascents and carried out scientific experiments in the area in the 1930s. The first Peruvian ascent was made by the brothers Yanac and their party. Less orthodox events on the summits have included the 1977 Rene Ghilini flight from its south summit on a hang-glider.

Peru's Mt Huascaran has twice been the scene of a major drama. In 1962 one of Huascaran's glaciers calved a 3 million-ton lump of ice about 300 m (1000 ft) from the summit that avalanched nine miles into the valley, destroying villages and killing 3000 people. Only eight years later, a 1970 earthquake (7.7 on the Richter scale) triggered another avalanche that detached a huge section of mountain, again from the north face of Huascaran. A mixed avalanche of rock and powder snow took off at 320 kph (200 mph) towards the valley. After clearing a high ridge the shockwave and the avalanche flattened the town of Yungay. Seventy thousand died and, in combination with the earthquake, a million

were made homeless. Even today, from a distance, it is possible to see the place where a huge chunk of the north face is missing. Palm trees grow forlornly from gaps in the lava and rubble that buried the town of Yungay – now completely rebuilt nearby.

Huascaran is the most popular peak in Peru, with six routes on the north peak and nine on the south peak, many on the 6 km (4 miles) long east face, which is a 900 m (3000 ft) ice wall topped by a 300 m (1000 ft) rock rampart. At least 29 have died on the peak, including 14 members of a Czech expedition unlucky to be climbing on 31 May 1970 when the massive avalanche/earthquake disaster destroyed Yungay. The most prolific climber in the Cordillera Blanca was Jaeger in 1977/78, during which time he made over a dozen solo ascents of the most challenging peaks. He spent 60 days alone at 6700 m (21,981 ft) on Huascaran, carrying out altitude research (he was a doctor). He died at 32 on Lhotse in 1980. In his memory the upper slopes of Huascaran were designated 'Glacier Jaeger'.

Despite the seemingly random dangers, Huascaran is still a magnet for international climbers, a 3000 m (9800 ft) ascent from the Callejon de Huaylas – four hours from Llanganuco. The normal route on the north face of Huascaran Norte is a fairly frequently attempted mix of ice, snow, rock and altitude. A superb rock route was put up by Moreno, Tomas and Valles (Via de los Catalanes) in 1983 in unusual conditions allowing rock boots to be worn most of the way. Another classic is the Barrard route (1973) on the north-east face, involving a 1600 m (5250 ft) ascent (10–14 hours), three bivouacs and a four-day round trip from base camp.

YERUPAJA, Peru (6634 m, 21,765 ft).

Yerupaja is also known as El Carnicero (the Butcher) after the sharp summit ridge, though its reputation would merit the name too. Yerupaja is the second highest mountain in Peru, with a west face of more than 1100 m (3600 ft).

It was first identified as one of the 6000 m (19,685 ft) peaks in the Cordillera Huayhuash by a 1927 survey party. A 1935 German-Austrian party had two near successes on it, reaching the shoulder of the south-west ridge. It was first climbed in 1950 by a party from Harvard, not without drama – one of the party lost all his toes from frostbite and the party made an emergency crevasse bivouac.

The next nine attempts all failed until a 1966 Alpine-style climb by Patterson and Peterek. Yerupaja Chico fell to Strum's party in 1967. In the last two decades, Yerupaja has attracted many famous mountaineers. Carrington and Rouse made a 1500 m (5000 ft) ice climb on the south face in 1977, as well as conquering the extreme rock and ice of the west face. Messner and Habeler made a new route on south-west Yerupaja Chico in only eight hours. It was Yerupaja that prompted Alan Rouse to describe the Cordillera Huayhuash as 'an excellent choice of classic routes and modern horrors'. The normal route is 15 hours from base camp at Laguna Carhuacocha (4138 m, 13,576 ft), reached on about day four of the Cordillera Huayhuash trek.

Peru is a fabulous mountain playground with over 20 ranges that would challenge the world's best. Alpine tactics are replacing expeditionary climbs. Lack of winter snow can hamper access, while snow clinging up to 70 degrees can be very loose. Ice flutings and unstable cornices add to the hazards.

ILLIMANI, Bolivia (6462 m, 21,201 ft)

Bolivia's highest peak overlooks the capital, La Paz, and was first climbed by the Alpinist Conway and his party in 1898. On the eastern side of Mt Illimani there is a dramatic precipice of some 1250 m (4000 ft) that Conway saw at night. '. . . the dim and vague horror of that almost fathomless plunge into the dark gulf at our feet was one of the experiences it has been worth living to know.' *Climbing in the Bolivian Andes*, Harper, 1901.

Illimani was the scene of a plane crash in 1938. Local gossip claims that the plane was laden with gold and the search for the wreckage has attracted bounty hunters. At one stage local suspicion of foreigners led to a Spanish party on the north ridge being fired on by Bolivian soldiers.

Access is by truck to Ventanilla or the Bolsa Negra, thence towards the Urania mine to the old bridge and ruin. From this point eight hours of fairly straightforward walking takes the climber to the 'condor's nest' (*El nid de condor*) on an interglacial ridge at about 5600 m (18,400 ft) where a camp can be made. The summit ridge is reached by passing either side of the icefall at about 6000 m (19,700 ft), by a relatively easy plod. There is now a road to the hut at 5014 m (16,450 ft). Club Andino Boliviano's Alfredo Martinez is the leading local guide. Settled weather is relatively predictable from May to September. The 6000 m (19,700 ft) peaks in this area require two to four days.

HUAYNA POTOSI, Bolivia (6088 m, 19,974 ft)

As 6000 m peaks go this is an easy one for those with basic ice-climbing experience. Full equipment will be needed for this very popular peak, which can be climbed in two to three days by an acclimatized party. Buses run regularly from La Paz to the Milluni mine via Alto La Paz. Eight kilometres (5 miles) from the mine, the Zongo pass is gained and, soon after that, the Laguna Zongo, where you can camp. Crossing the dam gives access to the glacier. Reasonable campsites can be found at 5600 m (18,400 ft) on the Campamento Argentino. From here, exercising caution with crevasses, the summit is some six hours away. Mist and wind are frequently encountered, but really bad weather is surprisingly rare on this peak, which makes it all the more attractive.

Much of our knowledge of the Cordillera Real comes from the German geologist Frederick Ahlfeld, who is said to have trekked some 100,000 km (60,000 miles) in the range, scaled most major peaks and formed the Club Andino Boliviano. Cordillera Real has recorded over 200 first ascents since 1960. Climbing is mostly on snow and ice about 5800 m (19,000 ft). Snow can be expected from October to April, but there is no particular climbing season.

ACONCAGUA, Argentina (6960 m, 22,834 ft) This, the highest peak of the Americas, is also known as Quechua (the White Sentinel). It is a convoluted peak whose easiest route, the west face, was conquered by the Swiss guide Matthias Zurbriggen and the Fitzgerald party of 1897. Fitzgerald turned back at 6700 m (21,980 ft), while Zurbriggen soloed the summit. The more difficult route is the south face, which was climbed Alpine style in 1954 by a French expedition, then one of the first 'big wall' climbs.

The sheer height of Aconcagua is even more impressive when one considers that it is only 150 km (93 miles) from the shore, and that only 100 km (60 miles) offshore the ocean bed plunges to 5667 m (18,590 ft) deep, reminding us that the Andes are the result of a tectonic plate boundary.

Unusual ascents include one by two priests in 1952, who carried a statue of Our Lady of Carmel to the summit. In 1934 two dogs are believed to have made the summit, probably a canine altitude record to outshine even the achievements of Tschingel, the dog that accompanied Coolidge's party on Pic Central de la Meije in the Dauphiné Alps.

Araucanian and Aymara Indians frequently visited the side of the mountain, and in 1985 an Inca mummy was found on the summit ridge, raising the possibility that the mountain was conquered by Indians long before Zurbriggen in 1897.

Puente del Inca (2718 m, 8917 ft), accessible by a 160 km (100 mile) bus journey from Mendoza, is the start of the climb. Here mules can be hired to haul equipment to base camp, carrying up to 60 kg (132 lb) each. After a couple of day's acclimatization, the 37 km (23 mile) walk to base camp at Plaza de Mulas 4400 m (14,436 ft) can be undertaken. Another two day's rest and acclimatization is recommended here, where there is basic crowded hut accommodation, before the next stage, seven hours by path to Refugio Antartida Argentina (5560 m, 18,241 ft) or the Berlin Hut (La Libertad) at 6000 m (19,685 ft). After yet more acclimatization (two days), a summit bid is possible from here but many take one more break at the Refugio Independencia at 6546 m (21,476 ft), possibly the world's highest hut. Six to nine hours should gain the summit from here, and in two days base camp can be regained.

Aconcagua is best climbed between mid-January and mid-February. Ten to fifteen days are usually necessary for the climb. The 'normal' (west face) route is strenuous and uninteresting, with a high fatality rate due to altitude, wind, cold, rockfalls, extreme dryness and dehydration. Over a hundred have died on Aconcagua in the last 60 years.

The two summits, north (6960 m, 22,834 ft) and south (6930 m, 22,736 ft) are joined by a 1 km (1000 yard) ridge (Cresta del Guanaco). The normal approach is up Quedabra de los Horcones to the Plaza de Mulas base camp at 4230 m (13,877 ft), Horcones Glaciar Superior and north ridge. The hardest routes are on the famous south face, first conquered in 1954 by a strong French party, taking nine days, four camps and the loss of many fingers and toes due to frostbite.

Climbing regulations are becoming more demanding in an attempt to minimize increasingly common accidents. A permit from the Sports Office at the Mendoza football stadium is required. Applications should be made in person, with a climbing plan, photos, doctor's certificate, ECG, and other formalities, allowing at least two days for processing. The Club Andinista Mendoza can help with details.

FITZROY, Argentina (3375 m, 11,072 ft)

*'Of all the climbs I have done,
the Fitz Roy . . . most nearly approached the
limits of my stamina and morale.'
Lionel Terray, after conquering Fitzroy.*

The Fitzroy range lies on the north-west shores of Lago Viedma, 240 km (150 miles) north of Calafate. Mount Fitzroy was named after the captain of the Beagle, the ship that in the 1830s carried Darwin around the world. Fitzroy goes by the name of Chaltén (God of Smoke) with the local Araucanian Indians, who believed it was a volcano because of its constant shroud of mist. The Indians were not prepared to upset their god by ascending him. Visitors have been put off by the remoteness of Fitzroy's sheer walls and its unpredictable raging storms. The first ascent of this, one of the great rock peaks in the world, came very late in 1952 by Magnone and veteran French climber Terray, whose exploits have included a first ascent of Makalu in the Himalayas. Three snowhole camps were used on the ascent. From the highest camp their summit bid took 40 hours, with a further bivouac on an icy ledge. In all the conquest was a five-week expedition during which one climber died – in a stream on the approach to the mountain.

The other famous peak, Cerro Torre (3128 m, 10,262 ft), was the scene of a disputed and now discredited summit bid attempt by Maestri and Egger who claimed ascents of the near vertical east and north faces. Egger was killed on the descent, and the photographic evidence was lost with him. Maestri claimed to have climbed it in two days with Egger in 1959, only a year after it defeated the great Bonatti, who said that only prolonged siege tactics would succeed. In the 1960s and 1970s many expeditions failed on Cerro Torre – British, Argentine, Japanese, Italian, Swiss and American.

Maestri returned in 1970, determined not to be defeated, with a drill powered by combustion engine, weighing about 150 kg (330 lbs). The aim was to drill and bolt their way up the face – hardly Alpine style or ethics! By June they had reached within 400 m (1300 ft) of the top, and returned in November to complete the route, but Maestri was again defeated by the summit ice wall. Their route had involved 800 m (2600 ft) of ice climbing, 800 m (2600 ft) of rock climbing and 365 m (1200 ft) of mechanically aided bolt placement. It was the latter that determined that this could not really be classed as a 'mountaineering' ascent. The first summit climb by accredited methods was made in 1974 by Ferrari's Italian party, which approached from the western ice-cap side.

CORDILLERA PAINE, Chile

This spectacular range lies 112 miles north of Puerto Natales, and to the south of the Cerro Fitzroy. The impressive Cerro Paine (3050 m, 10,006 ft) was first climbed in 1957. The Paine Horns have one of the highest rock walls in the world – the sheer east face of 1200 m (3936 ft), was first climbed by South Africans in 1974. In January 1963 a British party was the first to climb the central tower, followed a mere 20 hours later by a totally independent Italian party.

The Paine group has been the setting for many adventures and near disasters. The 1961 South Patagonia survey attracted great interest, not least for the atrocious weather encountered in these southerly latitudes. A British party with Whillans and Bonington nearly ended in disaster when Whillans' fixed rope broke, frayed by the wind. Bonington nearly died the next day when an abseil rope broke after he descended from the summit.

CHAPTER 11 Skiing

At the height of the European summer, the reverse seasons of the Southern hemisphere bring winter to the Andean snowfields in a ski season lasting from June to October. Skiing in the Andes is a very different experience from skiing in the Alps. South American countries lack the highly developed tourism infrastructure that we have come to expect in the Alps. Only three Andean countries claim to have ski resorts, and one of these (Chacaltaya, La Paz, Bolivia) really only qualifies by virtue of being (at 5200 m, 17,000 ft) the highest ski resort in the world.

> The best Andean skiing is located in an 1250 km (800 mile) part of the Chilean and Argentine Andes. Snowfields in the north are higher and have colder powder snow, while in the south resorts at a lower altitude occasionally provide the unflatteringly named 'Andean cement'.

Apart from pure adventure ski mountaineering, which is available on any snowfield in the Andes by shouldering skis and climbing, Andean resort skiing is confined to Argentina and Chile. While it would be wrong to propose an Andean ski trip as a viable alternative to an Alpine holiday (because of the time and distance involved), Andean skiing is an adventure for the better off skier in search of dramatic terrain and something new. Dolomitic scenery; micro-climates of perfect powder; pistes perhaps cleared by oxen; and flash rainstorms on lower slopes – all these make the skiing mostly unpredictable, but never dull.

ARGENTINA

Las Leñas

Las Leñas – Argentina's premier ski resort – has high season in July and August. The resort's claimed annual snowfall of 650 cm (250 inches) is perhaps optimistic – the Chilean Andes have had better snow in recent seasons – but Las Leñas' snow is reliable enough for many national teams to train there in our summer months. It is the first South American resort to gain World Cup accreditation and is the opening venue of the World Cup season.

Las Leñas was created in 1983 after the Falklands War. The purpose-built resort has the look one would expect from imported Franco-Swiss technology, with an exclusive, trendy up-market feel and prices to match its well-heeled Mendoza patrons. It lies in red-rock Dolomitic scenery above the natural treeline and above San Rafael in the appropriately named Valle Hermosa (beautiful valley), 250 km (160 miles) and three hour's drive south of Mendoza. Pistes go from 2250 m (7382 ft) up to 3400 m (11,253 ft) – highly respectable by Alpine standards, but only of middling altitude here in the Andes. The resort can sleep 300 visitors and claims to be able to shift 9000 skiers per hour through its lift systems. At peak season it can be uncomfortably busy.

Four first-class hotels, 305 self-catering apartments and convention-style facilities all open directly on to the pistes. The new Piscis Hotel has luxury accommodation for 200 with a European style casino and indoor-outdoor pool. A shopping arcade, restaurants, bars and a disco are conveniently placed for *après ski*. Slightly cheaper accommodation is available in the Hotel La Huenca, Los Molles, a 300 Austral (30 pence) bus ride from the resort.

Modest by Alpine standards, Las Leñas has a ski area of 40 sq km (15 sq miles). Eleven lifts serve 39 downhill runs, totalling 60 km (40 miles) providing 1200 m (4000 ft) of vertical descent and a longest continuous run of 8 km (5 miles). There are 16 km (10 miles) of cross country tracks as well as guided off-piste skiing, some of which is extreme. The main disadvantage of such a spectacular mountain range is the frequent strong wind that tends to close the higher lifts and turns the otherwise champagne powder to crust.

Moguls, gullies and motorway reds are rare, but there are some black runs worthy of the name – particularly the 40-degree Marte, which often carries 30 cm (1 ft) of light, flattering powder. Names of other runs are suitably celestial for a resort of such purpose-built lunar appearance – Venus, Neptuno, Vulcano, Minerva, Apolo – to name but a few. Three new chairlifts are being built for 1991.

Ski-hire equipment is excellent – modern and new. Ski school is also good, with English being widely spoken. Access is by plane to Buenos Aires (15 hours) plus a 90-minute internal flight to Malargue airport, followed by a 70 km (45 mile) bus transfer to the resort. As an example of 1990 prices, Journey Latin America have a one-week package to Las Leñas, including flights, half-board, lift-pass and transfers for £1297.

The most time-effective option is the Saturday to Saturday overnight trip, which gives five to six days skiing in the resort. The extravagance of skiing at £200 a day can be mitigated by extending the holiday and taking in some of the excellent side trips such as the Iguassu Falls, whale watching on the Valdez peninsula (September), or riding on the *gaucho estancias* (pampas ranches).

Bariloche

The winter season at San Carlos de Bariloche is from early July to early October. Bariloche hosts its early season snow carnival (*Fiesta de la Nieve*) and national ski championships each August. Early season crowds from Argentina and Brazil make for long lift queues and scarce accommodation. Except on the highest pistes, the snow can be unreliable, and August can be rainy on lower slopes. However, Bariloche's four bowls are generally good in September, especially at Cerro Catedral (14 km, 9 miles from town) where a new high lift will maximize natural snowfall.

Some 60 km (40 miles) of piste satisfy most standards of skier, with a longest run of 4 km ($2\frac{1}{2}$ miles). A 25-person cable car, nine double chairs, T-bars and pomas make for a claimed lift capacity of 20,000 per hour. As one might expect from this Swiss-style resort on the shores of Lake Nahuel, the *après ski* is fondue-based, but more than a splash of Latin tempo makes the night life memorable.

Cerro Chapelco

Four hours north of Bariloche, skiers can be assured of earlier nights, fewer queues, more moderate skiing and more reliable snow at Cerro Chapelco, near San Martin de los Andes. Many dub this the prettiest South American resort, with intermediate pistes running through mossy beech forests and fine views of the Lanín volcano and Lake Lacar towards Chile. The slopes are from 1250 m (4125 ft) to 1950 m

(6396 ft) with good snow most of the year and a longest run of 5.5 km (3.8 miles).

There are no hotels on the slopes, but San Martin is only some 10 km (6 miles) away and there are plans to expand the resort in the immediate area of the slopes. July and August are also to be avoided, unless you seek the crowds of the annual *Fiesta de la Nieve* on 5 August. Ski hire is available in San Martin, but beware of being overcharged if your Spanish is not good.

Other Argentinian resorts are Esquel, 30 minutes from Bariloche by plane, famous for its talcum-light powder, frequently marred by 60 kph (40 mph) winds even on 'calm' days. Best known as a spring resort, Esquel's season lasts well into October.

The southernmost cross-country ski resort in the world is Ushuaia, Tierra Del Fuego, where enthusiastic members of the Club Andino have organized trails through beaver forests from the hut restaurant at Valle Mayor.

BOLIVIA

Chacaltaya

High on altitude, low on everything else but one-upmanship, as ski resorts go this is a one-llama town. At 5200 m (17,000 ft) Chacaltaya is currently the world's highest resort. The ski season is September to April, comparable to the European Alps.

Situated only 35 km (20 miles) from the capital, La Paz, Chacaltaya epitomizes Bolivia and the Bolivian attitude to tourism and life. Few locals have the money or the interest to make the 90-minute journey by hair-raising rough road, and compared with European or even the best of the other South American resorts, the skiing is limited. The oxygen bottle, provided for unacclimatized visitors, is reported to be more often empty than not – an attitude that puts Bolivia years behind Europe and even its neighbours in the business of tourism.

Facilities are basic – some skis and equipment can be hired on weekends, hot drinks are available from the spartan restaurant. Two ski tows give access to a 200 m (600 ft) run from which departs the cliff edge. All but the very well acclimatized will need frequent rests between runs. Because of the relatively easy road access, this is a great place to experience altitude sickness, so proceed with caution.

Wear old clothes, since the ski tow has a habit of ripping them. Make sure you obtain a good hook with your rental equipment with which to attach yourself to the tow. The visitor will need to take an organized tour from La Paz, one of the best being from Club Andino, really only available at weekends. Despite Chacaltaya being unlikely to host the next Winter Olympics, it is still the highest in the world: the views over the Altiplano to Lake Titicaca and neighbouring peaks Illimani, Murarata and Huayna Potosi are magnificent. Skier or not, it is great to say you have been there.

CHILE

The Chilean season lasts approximately from May to October, but July and August are the best months. While there are a few short tows operating just 50 km (30 miles) from the capital, Santiago, the main skiing is at Portillo, in Aconcagua province, five hours by train from Santiago.

Portillo

Portillo's slopes are long (one of 10 km, 6 miles), hard (it has hosted World Championship events), varied and fast (venue for the 1978 world speed record – 205 kph, 128 mph) and high 2849 m (9348 ft). The resort has seven main runs, with plenty of off-piste powder.

Intermediate skiers will find plenty on the Plateau, the Juncalillo (1371 m, 4500 ft), the Enlace and the Nido de Condores. Roca Jack, the challenging black run, is only 850 m (2770 ft) long with one section of 350 m (1000 ft) that is a double black. An Austrian ski school operates here on adequate beginners' slopes.

Despite its qualification as an international resort, Portillo is fairly inward looking with a disappointing reputation of surcharging American and European visitors. Theft of unattended equipment from the slopes has also become prevalent. There is a 650-bed hotel near the resort on the shore of the glacial Laguna Del Inca, with several restaurants, a cinema, night-club and sauna.

Other Chilean ski resorts near Santiago include Farellones, with three blue runs, suitable for winter weekends; La Parva (five intermediate runs); Lagunillas (only two slopes but magnificent valley views on the road up) and El Colorado, which has shuttle bus connections to Farellones and La Parva to give all day skiing in the sun.

Away from the Santiago area, Chillán has five runs rising from thermal baths and volcanic springs, with a long 2500 m (8000 ft) double chair. At Villarica Volcano a new 550 m (1800 ft) chair opens spectacular views to a smoking volcanic cone. Also dramatic is the skiing on the slopes of the Llaima volcano in Los Paraguas National Park, where a 1.6 km (1 mile) long lift and two ski lodges give access to all year round skiing.

By far the most promising resort on the Chilean ski scene is Valle Nevado, some 64 km (40 miles) from the capital, an hour by road and just a few minutes by helicopter shuttle service. Valle Nevado has been designed by the developers of Les Arcs and some of its space-age buildings are reminiscent of French purpose-built resorts such as Les Arcs or Tignes.

Selling itself as the 'ski capital of the southern hemisphere', the resort currently boasts a modest 25 runs on 25 km (16 miles) of well-groomed piste served by nine modern lifts. The available ski domain of 22,000 acres has room for a total of 50 runs. When fully developed, the longest run is expected to be 16 km (10 miles) and the top station will be 5380 m (17,908 ft), exceeding Bolivia's Chacaltaya by 275 m (900 ft).

For children there is a special 'snow garden' in the centre of the resort where lessons and supervision by qualified monitors is available. Valle Nevado's full-service rental shop has everything from beginners' skis to surf and snowboards, monoskis, parapente and hang-gliding. Off-piste opportunities are extensive. Guided heliskiing is available – through untracked powder and across glaciers, many of which have never previously echoed to the swish of ski and the thump of headplant. If it lives up to its considerable promise, Valle Nevado can expect to become an internationally famous resort.

59. Cuzco, Peru. Campesino *in the city.*

Index

(figures in italics denote illustrations)